CONTENTS

African Origin of Biological Psychiatry

Seymour-Smith, Inc.

1990

"Black Dot" Part I-II, first appeared in *Uraeus: Journal of Unconscious Life* (1980, 1982). "Uraeus, From Mental Slavery to Mastership," Part I-IV, first appeared in *Uraeus: Journal of Unconscious Life* (1977, 1978). *"Symbolism of the Crown,"* first appeared in the *Journal of African Civilizations* (1985).

Front & Back Cover Photos: Lamy, Lucie, *Egyptian Mysteries: New Light on Ancient Spiritual Knowledge,* Crossword, N.Y., 1981
Spine Photo: Brier, Bob, *Ancient Egyptian Magic*, New York, N.Y. 1980.

First Edition

Library of Congress Catalogue-in-Publication Data
King, Richard M.D., 1946
  African Origin of Biological Psychiatry
      I. Title
90-060393
ISBN 0-9624889-2-5 (pbk)   0-9624889-3-3 (hbk)

Acknowledgements

I have been blessed by virtue of my long association with Dr. Alfred Ligon and Bernice Ligon, and it is to these two great ones, my spiritual parents, who raised me up, in their dedication to a briefly forgotten ancient way, that I give thanks. They are Master Teachers, who along with other Masters of this great tradition, teach that the soul can be set free by breaking the chains of dense material body, with a process of intense education. Thank you, our giants, from all your wild young students. Thank you a thousand-fold for our vessels of education: Black Gnostic Studies, Aquarian Spiritual Center, Aquarian Bookstore, in Los Angeles. Thank you for *Uraeus, The Journal of Unconscious Life,* where Uraeus Parts I-IV and Black Dot, Parts I and II were first published. Thank you for showing us that the very idea of the soul is not only a fantasy but also quite real in giving meaning to the struggles of life. Thanks for your lifetime of personal struggle and sacrifice in caring for all of us.

Knowing beyond knowing my great wife, Paulette, has stood beside me through it all and has been the truthful mirror to my soul. Thank you my precious soulmate. Equally, I know the love of my beautiful children, Kent, Khadi and Knef; my greatgrandfather, Nathan King and grandmother Ivory Williams. Stand tall my mother, Camille, father Louis, sisters Melanie and Michelle; brothers Wayne and Ivory. I extend my appreciation to a large group of immediate family and extended family of friends and institutions for all that you have done to nuture the birth of this book, including: The KM-WR Science Consortium, Inc., Dr. Yosef ben Jochannan, Hunter Adams, Dr. Patricia Newton, Malachi

Andrews, Kim Warnette, Melody Robinson, The Association for the Study of Classical African Civilizations, Dr. Carl Word, Ricky Williams, Kefa, Bill Jones and Rkhty Wimby Jones, The First World Alliance of New York, Dr. Francis Cress-Welsing, Dr. Lewis King, Fanon Research and Development Center, Carol Barnes, Dr. Issac Slaughter, Dr. Annette Kyle-Vega, The School of Ethnic Studies at San Francisco State University, Valerie Woodson, Susan Knox, Lola Coleman, Dr. William Boyd, Odoch and Khautar Hawkins, Dr. Phillip McGee, Julian and Raye Richardson and Marcus Bookstores, Dr. George Locke, Drs. George and Elain Brotherr, Dr. Howard Mason, "Cat" Thompson, Black Psychiatrists of Northern California, Black Psychiatrists of California, Black Psychiatrists of America, Dr. Carl Drake, Dr. Price Cobbs, Dr. Walter Sherrington, Dr. Billy Joner, Legrand Clegg, Ivan Van Sertima, Ashra Kwesi, Jordan High School of Watts California, Whitter College, University of California at San Francisco Medical Center. University of Southern California-Los Angeles Medical Center. Thank you all for supporting our struggle and struggling just because you love Us.

Richard D. King, M.D.

Preface

African Origin of Biological Psychiatry produces data pertaining to the diagnosis of genetic predispositions of historical Blackness. World experts in science have always clashed in debating the origin of man however, a Geneticist from the University of California in Berkeley, using gene analysis, recently asserted that, "all modern races derived from an African Woman." As far as biochemist are concerned, the genetic evidence for evolution of modern people is so conclusive that the counter arguments have no validity.

There is significant meaning and purpose when Dr. King says, "The deeper you go into your collective mind the Blacker it gets." The higher you go into the study of the Ancient pyramids the Blacker you'll focus.

Get ready for this book. I believe this work will become a classic in Biological Blackness and force you to look in the mirror to make cognitive changes. African Centric education must become a ritual, life force and fundamental process of liberation. Dr. Richard King's dedication to African research, history, healing and transformation brings new hope for collective, high performing African Centric life.

African Origin of Biological Psychiatry does not consist of static facts, but parallels the Dogon worldview in that it provides us with a workable understanding of something alive, viewed from a biological standpoint. "The Black mind establishes a network of equivalencies between all things by means of a system of symbols that involve practical and theoretical metaphysics which, on one hand explains the universe, thus responding to the innate need to understand, and on the other hand, forms the spiritual framework of men's lives (The Pale Fox)."

For most Americans and African Americans, the study of origins has been approached from a Eurocentric worldview. The affect of this worldview on African Americans has been the development of mental slavery. King's research brings provisions that may challenge the very existence of biological racism that european science established to control behavior. His research is in rhythm with Neely Fuller Jr's views on African American priorities:

> Each and every victim of racism should minimize the time and effort spent doing anything other than, thinking, speaking, and acting in a manner that helps to eliminate racism, and establish justice. Fear, frustration, malice and confusion that is caused by racism retards constructive research activity and intellectual exchange between the people of the known universe.

This work gives Black Americans and Black-White Americans a working plan to study and learn who we are. We are confused about who we are and what to do to access our inner self, our community self. Knowing who you are will help you to formulate a concept of 'you' that can be used to activate quantum ideas, internal holistic forces and your infinite spirit. Dr. King shows us the Brilliance of Blackness and how Black charges your electro-magnetic inner mind providing access to the translation of, and entry into the "collective unconscious memory bank."

Students and Scholars, you will need to find a community Black book store where the books referred to in King's references should be available. As the great historian, Dr. Cheikh Anta Diop, recommended when urging young American scholars to form university teams: "In the effort to confirm various ideas that I have advanced, instead of limiting yourself to a negative, sterile skepticism, you should be dazzled, if not blinded by the bright light of future discoveries." From The *African Origin of Civilization* to *Stolen Legacy* to the next millenneum, the African Man and Woman has always had a priviledged place in the Universe. Knowledge lies in knowing both man and woman, all things, the source of all dimensions of life. Since belief is nothing but a self confirming theory, read this work with an open "third eye". You will transform onto a higher plane of consciousness and propel, Beyond Science, to a higher creative Kemetic form--AMEN-RA.

Malachi Andrews, E., D.Ed
Professor, Department of Kinesiology
California, State University Hayward, California

PART ONE

Chapter One

BLACK DOT......BLACK SEED
Archetype of Humanity I

B lack Dot is an ancient symbol for blackness, it is the black seed of all humanity, archetype of humanity, the hidden doorway to the collective unconsciousness-darkness, the shadow, primeval ocean, chaos, the womb, doorway of life. This ancient symbol for blackness was the subject of intense scientific investigation over a period of 300 thousand years by profound ancient scientists who were themselves black in consciousness. A long line of highly intelligent scientists studied their own essence, and discovered a hidden doorway to their souls and spirits; a doorway to advanced laws and rhythms that span the universe. They discovered universal laws rooted in the black seed, feeding every dimension of time and space. These original titans found that all life came from a black seed, all life was rooted in blackness, and all things possessed a memory of their collective ancestors.

Blackness, the universal solvent of all, was seen as the one reality from which life's loom spun. All colors, all vibratory energies were but a shade of black. Black was the color of the night sky, primeval ocean, outer space, birthplace and womb of the planets, stars and galaxies of the universe; black holes were found at the center of our own galaxy and countless other galaxies. Black was the color of carbon, the key atom found in all living matter. Carbon atoms linked together to form black melanin, the first chemical that could capture light and reproduce itself. The chemical key to life and the brain itself was found to be centered around black neuromelanin. Inner vision, intuition, creative genius, and spiritual illumination were all found to be dependent upon pineal gland blood; born chemical messengers that controlled skin color and opened the hidden door to the darkness of the collective unconscious mind, allowing the ancient priest-scientist to visualize knowledge from the mind's timeless collective unconscious memory banks. Indeed, Black Dot was found to be the hidden doorway to universal knowledge of the past, present and future. Presently, black people are awakening from the spell of mental slavery, ignorance of self, and an inability to spiritually focus the mind. *Black people have learned that a major key to shattering the chains of mental slavery is to know one's own history.* When one knows the true fullness of the ancestor's achievements then that person will believe that they can do the same today. When one knows what the ancestors did to develop themselves, in order to make such great advances, then they will know how to do the same today. For the ancestor and today's black person are literally the same person: king, queen, architect, physician, teacher, artist, competitor, merchant, jurist, and military giant. In knowing one's history one can expand the mind through the illusion of time and space, unite with ancient black priest-scientist ancestors, and utilize the same timeless and universal ideas to produce the same greatness.

Today's reborn black, mental masters can focus the mind by embracing their historical blackness, developing a deep knowledge of one's black ancestry and thereby *becoming fluent in the translation of ancient images* that appear in today's world. As a result, dreams and visions of the great but seemingly impossible, will be brought into reality rather than ignored, just talked about, or partially developed. No longer will one submit to an "I can't do attitude" but one of "I will do," "I will make this life perfectly beautiful and I won't stop until it is that way." "I will be my true Self."

Also, as men of today *again* stand on the threshold of the blackness of outer space they are forced to an awareness of the blackness of inner space. The advanced laws of nature required for understanding outer space, and the experience of space travel will bring up many collective unconscious memories, if poorly understood, will create illusions of grandeur, illusions of persecution, false barriers between brothers, and deadly relationships between nature and humanity. Certainly a racist, or sexist person who is by definition both egocentric and ethnocentric, crazily attempting to conquer nature, at war with the universe will be overwhelmed by the infinite blackness of outerspace and innerspace. These people would rather destroy the world than find the Black Dot, hidden doorway that allows one to become one with nature, in rhythm with the universe, by using the accumulated wisdom of one's ancestors contained within the mind. Thus, reborn black people carry upon their shoulders the salvation of humanity, the revitalization of a human family that is lost, unable to find the hidden doorway to a spiritual unity with nature. The Black Dot is the hidden doorway of life which again is the doorway through which a reborn people must pass.

The Black Dot...Defined

Blackness, as symbolized by the Black Dot, is the seed of humanity, the archetype of humanity, the black hidden doorway of historical unity with one's ancestors. Webster's dictionary defines seed as "the source, origin or beginning of anything; the part of a flowering plant that contains the embryo and will develop into a new plant; if sown, and fertilized and developed into ovule (new seeds)." Archetype, is defined as the original model from which all other things of the same kind are made. Thus, archetype and seed are synonymous, both referring to the origin, the basic model of humanity upon which the race is patterned. Archetype means seed and is one of the ancient African names for seed. Archetype is composed of two main words arche and type. Type is defined as a person, thing or event that represents or symbolizes another, especially another that is to come; the general form, structure, plan, style characterizing or distinguishing member of a class or group. Arch is defined as main, chief, principle; a curved structure used as support over an open space as in a doorway.

The human type's distinguishing characteristics is the mind, the ability to think, the ability to profit from history, from the accumulated experiences and wisdom of one's ancestors, collective unconscious. Thus, Black Dot is the seed archetype, a main doorway through which collective unconscious ideas pass as they become conscious.

C.G. Jung, took the term "Archetype' from the *Corpus Hermeticum* (Scott Hermetica, Vol. I, 140, 12b) and from Chap.2, Par. 6, of the De Divinis nominibus of Dioysius the pseudo Areopagite, which reads: But someone may say that the seal is not the same and entire in all its impressions. The seal, however, is not the cause of this, for it imparts itself wholly and alike in each case, but the difference in the participants make the impressions unlike, although the archetype is one, whole and the same (Jacobi, 1971). Jung was drawn to the term archetype most of all by the writings of the African scholar, St. Augustine who was a student of the Ancient African University. St. Augustine's ideae principales, 'For the principal ideas are certain forms, of stable and unchangeable reasons of things, themselves not formed, and so continuing eternal and always after the same manner, which are contained in the divine understanding. And though they themselves do not perish, yet after their pattern everything is said to be formed that is able to come into being and to perish. But it is affirmed that the soul is not able to behold them, save it be the rational soul' (Jacobi, 1973).

Black was used extensively by ancient Africans to represent a host of concepts, all of them having in common the idea of seed, and doorway to the collective unconscious mind including: the Egyptian hieroglyph for the Egyptian god Ra, the Sun, or Horus risen (Budge, 1969; Churchward, 1978); the result of the synthesis of the male principles (logical, left brain) and female principles (emotional, right brain); the African's great lakes holy land "Khui Land," birth place of humanity and home of the Twa People (King, 1978); North pole star and seven glorious ones of the Pleaides system; Star at the summit of the cone; the all seeing eye of Horus (Churchward, 1978), representative of the god like powers of inner vision, developed in the highest grade of the African University, Sons of Light (James, 1976). All black structures are used with the same symbolic meaning of hidden doorway to the collective unconscious. For instance, the Black stone of the Ka'ba of Mecca; Black stone of Pessinus, stolen from Hannibal's city of Carthage to Rome in the last Punic War; all Black Pyramidion; the black capstone usually found at the apex of pyramids, which were themselves symbolic of the mind, Ptah, and the hill that arose from chaos (conscious awareness, doorway, to the collective unconscious); The internal structures of the Great Pyramids of Khufu being symbolic of the all black world of Amenta (Massey, 1973; Churchward, 1978). The upper most chamber of the Great Pyramid, the Kings chamber is an all black room again symbolizing inner vision, the all seeing eye of Horus, Black Dot doorway to the collective unconscious (King, 1979; Jochannan, 1980). Concerning the Black cubit, Kamel Oshman Ghalet Pasha wrote in, *The Nilometric Cubit,* the Bulletin de la Societe Royale de Geographic Vol. 21, (1943) "The Black cubit of Ancient Egypt was of unknown origin. This cubit was carved on the Socle of the black granite colossus to the east of the entrance leading from the court of Ramses to the great colonade, and is found only on black stones or on what corresponds to their symbol. Its measured length is 54cm. R.A. Schwaller de Lubicz (1977) recently remeasured the black cubit and found its mathematical length to be 54.02376cm."

Humanities Ancestral Blackness-The Black Seed

The basic model upon which humanity is patterned is clearly an African model as proven by the abundance of archaelogical records that report humanoid remains in Africa of 9-12,000,000 million years old, including human foot prints that have been found in Ethiopia preserved in volcanic ash flows. Whereas, no skeletal remains older than 500,000 years have been found outside of Africa, the oldest reported finding was in Java, where a 500,000 year old human skeleton named Homo erectus (also called Java man) was discovered. In the Great Lakes region of Africa, numerous human skelatal remains have been found that are in excess of three million years old. It is believed that so called modern man, homo sapiens, evolved from homo erectus which in turn evolved from homo habilis which decended from the early primate ramapith-erectus. Albert Churchward (1978) suggests that homo erectus is actually the so called Pygmy or the Twa people, and that all humanity are children of the African Twa people. Thus, the vast majority of humanity's time on earth, many millions of years, was spent in a Black African context.

African Ancestral Blackness

The human family is a Black family, a Black race millions of years old that originated in Africa. According to African Historian, Dr. Ben Jochannan, the ancient Egyptians clearly defined their African origin in the papyrus of Hunefer, "We came from the beginning of the Nile where God-Hapi dwells, at the foothills of the mountain of the Moon." Dr. Ben Jochannan's interpretation of this ancient record, "The mountain of the moon," identifies Kenda's Kilimanjaro (a Kenya-base Ki Swahili word created by the indigenous Africans) and or Uganda's "Rwenzori Mountain." The Egyptians originated from Africa, south of the Sahara. Recent diggings and artifacts throughout Meroe, Ta-Nehisi, Itiopi, all of these south of Egypt, have further supported the southern origin of the Egyptians, black, white, red, brown or technicolor. The ancient Silt pyramids built around the Sebellian I,II and III period, or CA 250,000 to 6000 years BC in southern Ta-Merry and Ta-Nehisi also support the southern origin of the Egyptians. This is one of the reasons why Pharoahs went back south for their own "Sacred" or Holy "Burial Place" in the Valley of the Kings at Luxor (Jochannan, 1980).

Also, Albert Churchward and Wallis Budge have shown that the oldest Egyptian god was Bes, an African Pygmy or Twa person. "Bes here has the same type of face as the Pygmy," the first god anthromorphically depicted; it is the primitive human form of Horus I, Bes-Horus being the earliest type of the Pygmy Ptah. The human type was not given to any before Ptah, so that (Bes) shows that the ancient Egyptian left an indelible proof in their mythology of their decent from the first human, which was the Pygmy. These little people have some of the principle features of the earliest mythology of old Egypt. Bes, who was at a later date made to represent a type of Horus I, was at first their "Chief of the Nomes," and it was from these Pygmies that the first mythology of Egypt sprung. All have been brought on, added to, and made use of in the various types; from the earliest mythos-astronomical, stellar, lunar, and solar mythologies to the Eschatology. Thus we find out that they come from the south of the land of Punt (today's Somali Republic, parts of Republic of Kenya, and Republic of Tanzania-Northeast Africa).

In regards to the homeland of the ancient Pygmy of Twa people, Maspero said that "all that lay beyond Punt was a void or intermediate boundary land between the world of men and that of the gods-the island where the living came into contact with the souls of the departed..."Khui Land."

The Holy Land of the ancient Egyptians was named Holy because it was the birthplace of man. The Khui Land, great lakes region of Africa at the head of the Nile, is the birthplace of the ancestors of the Egyptians; the so called Pygmy or Twa People, parent of all humanity. This is the same site where current science has found the oldest human skeletal remains in the world. The source of the Nile-Equatorial provinces were the great lakes. The lakes and papyrus swamps were the Ta-Nutter, or Holy Land-i.e., "the Land of the Spirits or Gods". The sky as the Great Celestial water was divided into two great lakes, one to the north (Lake of Kharu), and one to the south (Lake of Ru); Book of the Dead CVII-CVL.

All of today's human forms: African, Asian, European, Latino, and

Oceanic, are very recent children of their black african parents, the Twa people. All humanity started in Africa and then migrated to the different corners of the globe, changing in superficial aspects as a result of different climatic-sunlight exposure conditions. All humanity has a vast black origin, Black Dot, in Black North East Africa. Clearly European-Africans must not forget Europe's first historian, Herodotus, who said that "the Egyptians, Colchians, Nubians, and Ethiopians have thick lips, broad nose, wooly hair and are burnt of skin" (Jochannan, 1971).

Concerning the relationship of changes in skin color to changes in the sunlight as the result of migrations to Europe and cold glacial cycles, Bernard Cambell sites in his book, *Humankind Emerging,* "It seems likely that Austrolpitheus and early tropical Homo eretus as well, had been quite dark skinned." In equatorial Africa dark color is an advantage. Overexposure to the ultra violet rays of the tropical sun is harmful to skin, and many experts feel that as the hominid skin became less hairy and more exposed, the melanocytes (cells that produce the skin darkening pigment melanin) compensated by producing extra pigment to block the ultra violet rays. The presence of a screen of pigment inhibits the photosynthesis of vitamin D in the skin. When people settled permanently in regions with less sunlight they did not get enough vitamin D; in this case pigment was no longer a protection but a drawback. The problem was exacerbated by the onset of cold. The well fitted hides worn against the cold decreased the amount of sunlight that could fall upon the skin. A degree of pigmentation that could further the contribution of vitamin D to the body's chemistry was better for survival, so lighter skin evolved. In this way we can account for the evolution of the blond northerner (white-European-African). Today, we know that man is unable to obtain the vitamin from any terrestrial foods, either vegetable or animal, but that fish oils contain vitamin D and fish can be eaten as a substitute for exposure to sunlight. Furthermore, we have learned that a deficiency of the vitamin causes the bone bending disease named rickets. We find many skeletons of Neanderthals (human forms that evolved from Homoerectus), Twa people, and especially children having rickets, showing direct evidence of a deficiency of vitamin D. It is equally surprising that among the Cro-Magnon people, who succeeded Neanderthals in these icy regions, and whom we know to have had fishing tackle, the incidence of rickets is greatly reduced. The importance of sunlight to the survival of early Homo Sapiens in northern lands, and the limitations that it placed on his expansion cannot be exaggerated. Thus, numerous European Neanderthals skeletal findings of rickets is critical physical evidence that the first people in Europe were black skinned. These Africans developed bone deformations in the minimum sunlight ice age, because their dark skin reduced the amount of vitamin D produced in skin thereby reducing calcium levels for bone growth.

As African people migrated to different parts of the world they used the stars of the sky to guide them to their travels. Over a period of many thousands of years and multiple exoduses from Africa, careful scientific observations of the north pole star were repeatedly used as a very important direction finder. Also, changes in the north pole star were noticed to coincide with gravitationally induced changes in the earth's geological cycles (floods, earthquakes) and in weather cycles (glacier cold spells and tropical warm spells). During periods of glacial conditions, the northern continents were literally frozen and African people who survived in such climates over thousands of years changed in skin color from black skin to white skin due to the relationship of reduced sunlight, skin melanin, vitamin D and dietary calcium. Thus, the eye on the mount, or the Black Dot, or point within the center of the circle was the earliest law in heaven, the judge, all seeing eye that governed major changes in humanity, geological change, African exoduses (world wide human migrations), weather cycles and human physical-physiological changes. Black Dot, the eye of the mount representing the north pole star direction finder was known as Anup or Horus in Egypt, Sydik in Phoenicia, Anu in Babylonia, Tai-Yih in China, Avather or Zivo in Mesopotamia, Ame-No-Foko-Tachi-Kami in Japan and various other names in different parts of the world.

Black Dot Doorway To The Collective Unconscious

Just as there are written and geological records of humanities' past there are biological and mental records of humanities' origin. The collective is that part of the human mind which contains the mental records of one's ancestors and is that body of knowledge developed by our ancestors and accumulated over millions of years. The libraries of our mind are infinite, and contain the wisdom of all man's past, present, and even the future unity of universal knowledge, universal life.

The hallmark of humanity was the mind. The mind stored the ability to think, to observe, measure, theorize and thereby communicate with nature. The mind was indeed the reservoir of millions of years of African experience in science, medicine, art, religion, architecture, military psychology, culture, and magic, all forming the collective unconscious core upon which all humanity was patterned. Thus there is only one race of humanity on this planet earth, the Black Race, with many shades of Black, From Black-Black to Black-White. All members of the human family may have various shades of skin color but they are all rooted in Blackness.

The critical question, then, is how to relate to one's blackness. Needless to say, there are a variety of examples of how people relate to their historical blackness.   Some examples include racism, mental slavery, outright denial of blackness, avoidance of black ancestry, and a general fear of being overwhelmed by blackness. Most people today are lost because they continue to avoid their historical black selves. All people must answer the complex question of blackness for themselves, but certainly Black people today, the victims of centuries of racism must uplift themselves to fully understand that racist people, those who reject their own blackness, will not find the hidden doorway, or Black Dot. Therefore they will remain lost and extremely dangerous.

Ancient African Philosophy of Blackness

The Memphite Theology according to African Historian, George G.M. James, is inscribed on a stone now kept in the British Museum. It contains the philosophical views of the Egyptians from the predynastic period before 4,000 B.C. In Part I, precreation is represented as follows:

> "The Primate of the Gods Ptah, conceived in his heart every-
> thing that exists and by his utterance created them all. He is
> first to emerge from the primeval waters of Nun in the form
> of a primeval hill. Closely following the hill, the god Atom also
> emerges from the waters and sits upon Ptah. There remains
> in the waters four pair of male and female gods: (1) Nun and
> Naunet-the primeval waters and the counter heaven; (2) Huh
> and Hauhet-the boundless and its opposite; (3) Kuk and Kau-

ket-darkness; (4) Amun and Amaunet-the hidden and it's opposite. Memphite Theology contained ten principles: four pairs of opposite principles, together with two other gods: Ptah representing Mind, Thought, and Creative Utterance; while Atom joins himself to Ptah and acts as Demiurge and executes the work of creation.

This critical account reveals that Africans discovered the concept of Atom thousands of years before Europe. Additionally, Africans first defined the concept of mind or psychology, and what is today known as the four powers: strong nuclear forces, weak nuclear forces, electromagnetism and gravity. However, it was Ptah or the mind that was the primate (first, chief, main) god that arose out of the primeval waters of chaos (collective unconscious).

Ancient Egyptians built pyramids as a symbolic image of the hill, Ptah rising out of the primeval waters of earth. The capstone of the pyramid, the pyramidion, was usually an all black granite obesidan stone. Then too, in the case of the upper most King's chamber of the great pyramid of Khufu at Ghizeh is a room in which all four walls, ceilings and floors are black granite stone in color. Thus, the god Ptah is pictured as Black in color. Ptah being defined as the primate of Gods again signifies how the mind is the chief link to the primeval ocean, chaos and collective unconscious. The fact that the apex of the hill was black again shows how ancient Africans considered blackness to be the primate or main doorway to the collective unconscious. Knowledge of black ancestral history provided the access to and the translation of the collective unconscious memory banks.

The internal structure of the Great Pyramid of Khufu was symbolic of the all black underworld of Amenta, the all black doorway to the collective unconscious. Passage through Amenta, or the development of blackness, produced: an expansion of consciousness (inner vision), spiritual consciousness, illumination, unity with nature, an activated pineal gland, creative genius, godlike powers attained by man on earth, or the functional development of the extrasensory powers. Gerald Massey has recorded, "The entrance to the Great Pyramid was concealed by means of a movable flagstone that turned on a pivot which none but the initiated could detect. It was known as the door or the stone that revolved when the magical word or 'open Sesame' was spoken. Thus

Horus was the door in the darkness (blackness), the way where no entrance was seen, the life portrayed for the manes in death; the first door of twelve in the passage of Amenta. These twelve are described in the book, *The Coming Forth by Day, Book of the Dead.* The twelve divisions correspond to the twelve hours of darkness during the nocturnal journey of the sun. The first division has no visible door or entrance. The rest have open doors, and the twelfth has double doors. It is hard to enter, but made easy for the exit into the land of eternal life. Here is the mystery: how to enter where there is no door and the way is all unknown? It is explained to the manes how divine assistance is to be obtained. When the strains of life on earth are effaced, strength is given for forging the entrance where there is no door and in that power the manes penetrates with or as the god."

How to Conceptualize the Black Dot Today

How can one become aware of the Black Dot, the doorway to the collective unconscious? Clearly one must study deeply African history and one must know and utilize the ten virtues and seven liberal Arts that are defined in George G. M. Jame's *Stolen Legacy.* Where do we start? We start by developing our character and becoming focused on our own development. Literally one becomes capable of using feelings to extract knowledge from the collective ancestral memory banks. For, as defined in the Memphite Theology, Ptah, the mind, conceived in his heart feelings. The feelings (intuitional-emotional tones) are key tools that must be developed to grasp the ideas in the collective unconscious world of chaos and pass it through the Black Dot doorway over into the world of conscious awareness. "When the strains of life are effaced" one develops the strength to open the hidden Black doorway to find the needed knowledge to solve seemingly impossible tasks; to develop perfection and to fullfill our highest creative dreams. It was through the use of the Ten Virtues, Negative Confessions and Seven Liberal Arts, that the heart was developed and character strengthened. Certainly, it is the lack of character among many black people today that produces so much disunity, petty personality conflicts, excessive paranoia among black people, poorly tuned and unpredictable emotional flashes. A strong heart will yield a strong character and emotional balance, thus let's consider the daily use of the Ten Virtues, the first two being: (1)

control of thought and (2) control of action (emotion). Ask yourself the next time you feel emotional about something: does the feeling make logical sense, ask questions in order to gather knowledge of both sides of the issue, know your emotional blind spots and tendencies to distort reality. Virtues (1) and (2) combined are defined as justice (feel deeply, listen to your heart, balance feelings with logic, logic with feelings). Reality must both make sense logically and feel right emotionally.

Black Dot is an ancient African symbol for blackness, the black seed of all humanity. Black Dot is the hidden doorway to the collective unconscious mind the ancestral memory bank for all. The use of the collective unconscious as the hallmark is the distinguishing attribute of humanity. Present day humanity comes from the Black African race developed over a period of many millions of years. Black Dot represents the origin of all humanity. All Africans, Europeans, Latinos and Asians came from the same black womb of the black woman fertilized by the black seeds of the black man. The ancestral memory bank (collective unconscious) is a collection of African experience and wisdom thereby requiring a profound grasp of African history and a Black approach for the efficient translation of ancient African images in today's world.

Humanity may differ in outer appearance, with variations of colors but internally they are all black, all African at the core. The question for all humans is how to relate to this blackness. A transformation process requires, first, the right heart or feelings and profound African knowledge as taught in ancient African universities. Today's racist is afraid, ignorant of his/her blackness, choosing to run from the ancestral black core. Today's reborn black masters will accept their blackness, become unified with the universe and be inspired to creative genius at levels that surpass the pyramids. Uraeus is the symbol of the transforming energy for the soul. Black dot defines the hidden doorway to the collective unconscious; primeval waters, universal forces that nourishes all life forms, and the hidden doorway through which the transforming soul-energy of Uraeus passes.

Chapter Two

BLACK DOT......BLACK SEED
Archetype of Humanity II

   G eorge James (1976) reported that, the education of the Egyptian Priest consisted of specialization in secret systems of language and mathematical symbolism called hieroglyphics. This system was used by the Priest, in order to conceal secret and mystical meaning of their doctrines. The mystery system of Egypt employed modes of spoken language which could be understood only by the initiated. These consisted of myths, parables, and a secret language called Senzar. Egyptians attached numerical values to word letters and to geometrical figures, to perform the same mystical function as hieroglyphics. Each temple was to be a microcosm and symbol of the universal temple, as well as a reproduction of the world. According to Herodotus, the Egyptian Priests possessed supernatural powers, for they had been trained in the esoteric Philosophy of the Greater Mysteries, and were experts in magic. Egyptian Priests were the first genuine Priests of history who exercised control over the laws of nature. Magic was used as applied religion and primitive scientific method.

   The amulet of the Eye-of-Horus is an excellent example of ancient Egyptian's reference to the Black Dot, it's deeper meaning and truth, concealed with myth, geometrical and mathematical symbolism. One of the most important myths of ancient Egypt concerned Horus. Regarding this myth, Bob Brier (1980) writes, "According to myth, Horus fought his evil uncle Seth to avenge the death of his father Osiris. In battle, Horus' eye was torn to pieces, but with magic, Thoth, god of writing, assembled the pieces. Each element of the Eye-of-Horus represented a different fraction; the hieroglyph for 1/2 was, 1/4 and so on. The total of the fractions is 63/64, the missing 1/64 is supposedly supplied magically by Thoth. The amulet was called Udjat or 'Sound Eye' because of its association with the regeneration of Horus' eye."

The eye of Horus is thus the third eye, a regenerated or transformed eye, the eye of magic. Close examination of an eye of Horus, reveals that the Black Dot is the pupil or 1/4 and it is the point through which light enters the eye. Through the process of initiation, psychological integration, expansion of consciousness, and translation of the unconsciousness, the ancient African Mystery School student, through a process of initiation, passed from a state of the lower self awareness, small case eye (i), into the Higher Self (I). Capital I also refers to the column or backbone in the human body, temple, which contains a string of glands along the column, with each higher gland yielding progressively greater hormone output. This progresses with the pineal gland, or third eye, at the top of the spinal column and culminates with the development of an expanded state of consciousness. Again, George James reported that, The earliest theory of salvation was the Egyptian theory. The Egyptian Mystery System had as its most important object, the deification of man and taught that the soul (mind) of man, if liberated from its bodily fetters, could enable him to become godlike, attain vision and hold communion with the immortals, (sons of Light).

Black Dot Pyramidion, Doorway to The Temple

There are a number of examples that illustrate that the ancient Egyptians concealed their inner knowledge in the construction of architectural monuments. Before the entrance to the Egyptian temple there usually stood two obelisks, with the most important part being the pyramidial point or pyramidion. The pyramidion has been found by modern science to often be an all black capstone at the top of most pyramids and obelisks. The entrance to the temple-obelisk's highest point was black, thus it was the first point of the pyramid-temple site or obelisk-temple site to receive sunlight as the sun arose from darkness on each new day. The black pyramidion and the Eye-of-Horus referred to a doorway of darkness, (pyramidion, pupil) where light first penetrates when entering the temple or human body. However, it is not until one examines modern scientific literature that one can fully appreciate this ancient African reference to black, sunlight and the night eye.

Black Dot Locus Coeruleus - Doorway To The Temple

The brain structure, locus coeruleus, offers strong biological scientific evidence that directly support the Ancient African claim that Black Dot is the doorway to the temple, the mind and collective unconscious. First, The Name Locus Coeruleus Literally Means Black Dot. Locus is a latin word, stlocus locum, meaning point or dot. Coeruleus is derived from the Indian Sanskrit name caeruleus yamas, meaning Black. This is a critical finding because the Sanskrit name, caeruleus, appears to predate Greek, Latin or other Western European languages. In fact this name appears to be of African origin and was used by Africans in Africa, Europe and Asia. It appears that Ancient European Sanskrit borrowed the term from the African populations that migrated to India from Africa many thousands of years earlier. The profound and excellent journal by current day Afrikan Hebrews, *History, the Bible and the Blackman,* (1980) recently reviewed the book *Ethiopia: The Missing Link in African History* by Rev. Sterling Means (1945). His book cited many reports of the Black population of India that begins at the southern side of the Hindoo-Kush mountains. "The place where the Ethiopian race formed into the Hindu or Indian Nation. India was first peopled by a Black Race, with whom Herodotus was acquainted under the name Ethiopians. The continent (India) is over one-third Negroid today." "The earliest people to occupy India are supposed to belong to the Negritic Race." Herodotus states that, The Ethiopian race inhabited the lands towards the rising and setting sun. He divided them into two nations and said they differed in nothing from the other Ethiopians save their language and the character of their hair. The Eastern Ethopians have straight hair while those of Libya (Africa) are more woolly than any other nation on earth. The Ancient Empire of Ethiopia once included all the subcontinent of India. "The Statue of Buddha with Negroid features is found throughout India which shows that a woolly haired race once ruled there" (Dury, Vol. 1). Thus, the name caeruleus, though Indian Sanskrit, is a borrowed African word.

Additional proof of the African origin of caeruleus can be found in the work of the great African historian, Cheikh Anta Diop (1978), in *The Cultural Unity of Black Africa,* concerning early African settlers of Greece. Diop states that, "Danaus had a wife named Ethiopis and a daughter Celeno, whose name means Black (a daughter of Atlas also bore the same name). Celeno had a son by Neptune called Celenus. Celenus, son of Phylos, is the basis for the ancient legendary cults of Pelopinnosus. Perseus, the King of Argos, had a grandson Celesus (Celena was also the daughter of Proteus), the King of Tiryus. The Indian Sanskrit word coeruleus is derived from the Ancient Ethiopian name, Celeno, which means Black. This is further proof of the word's Ethiopian origin, because the Greeks borrowed their mythological figures from the Ethiopians (Jochannan 1974, 1980). Dr. Ben Jochannan has found, "Hercules, whom the Greeks admitted was one of the Gods, was of Ethiopian origin".

Certainly in the historical study of Black Dot, locus coeruleus is one of the most important subjects to explore. Locus coeruleus literally means Black Dot. We have reviewed the evidence that coeruleus is an Indian Sanskrit name borrowed from Ethiopians in India and that it came from the Ethiopian word CELENO. Thus, we are left with this extraordinary evidence that ancient Africans studied brain anatomy and named this critical brain site coeruleus. Celano, because of its appearance and function, was symbolically in line with other research evidence of the time. As western science investigates the locus coeruleus, increasingly more biological evidence emerges that directly supports the ancient African concept that coeruleus is a Black Dot doorway to the collective unconscious.

The locus coeruleus is black because it contains large amounts of melanin, the same chemical that produces skin color (Amaral 1977, 1978). Its cells provide the principle noradrenergic nerve supply to many areas of the brain, cerebral cortex, hippocampus, cingulate gyrus, and amygdala areas that make up the major portion of the limbic cortex. The locus coeruleus also supplies part of the norepinephrine found in other brain areas such as hypothalamus, thalamus, habenula (deep pineal), cerebellum-lower brain stem and spinal cord (Kobayashi, 1975). Importantly, the locus coeruleus affects memory, as one would expect because melanin affects memory. The locus coeruleus is normally involved in the temporal delineation of the susceptibility period of newly formed memory. A malfunction of the locus coeruleus can result in a profound extension of the normal susceptibility period of newly formed memory to ECS-produced amnesia (Zorentzer, 1976). Additional evidence of the role of the locus coeruleus as a doorway to the collective unconscious is present in the biological evidence that the locus coeruleus is the uppermost point in an all black neuromelanin nerve tract that runs from the brain stem into the spinal cord. Olszneki (1964) mapped the brain stem and found 12 brain sites containing pigmented (melanin) cells. These are the substantia nigra with its associated nucleus brachialis pigmentosus and nucleus paranigralis. The other nine nucelii are either part of a neuro-melanin column or adjacent to the neromelanin column that Bazelon (1967) found. Marsden (1961) and Scherer (1939) have found that melanin is present in the brain of all animals, with the degree of pigmentation increasing as one moves up the evolutionary ladder. Mammals have the greatest degree of pigmentation among all animals, and primates have the greatest brain intensity pigmentation among all of mammals. With primates, the higher the evolutionary type of brain organization or the closer the primate to the human type, the greater the degree of pigmentation within the brain (Cotzias, 1974). Scherer (1939) reported that in humans the intensity of pigmentation of the locus coeruleus was the same as that found in the substania nigra; deep melanin pigmentation. This was in contrast to the near human type primate, chimpanzee, where the substania nigra is highly pigmented, but the locus coeruleus is pigmented much less.

Thus, all animals have an internal core of melanin in their brains. *All humans possess this Black internal brain evidence of their common Black African Origin. The All Black neuromelanin nerve tract of the brain is profound proof that the human race is a Black race, with many variations of Black, from Black-Black to White-Black, all internally rooted in a vast sea of Brain Blackness.* One of the critical keys that distinguishes man from all other animals is this presence of intense blackness, neuromelanin pigmentation of the locus coeruleus, Black Dot, the upper most center of pigmentation, the doorway that opens into an all black hall of blackness, the neuromelanin *"Amenta"* nerve tract.

Black Dot Black Ectoderm, Doorway To The Temple

There is only one race of humans on this planet earth, the Black Race, with many nuances of Black. Just as there are written and geological records of humanities' past there are also biological and mental records of humanities' origin. After the male sperm fertilizes the female egg, it divides and multiplies to form an early cluster of cells, blastula, from which the fetus child will develop. This early blastula contains three layers, outer ectoderm, and inner layer endoderm and mesoderm. Every part of the body has its origin in one of these three layers of cells. The outer layer of the ectoderm contains melanin throughout its outermost layer (Pearse, 1976). By the 28th hour following conception fertilization of the female egg, the ectoderm has begun to invaginate into the interior of the cluster of early fetal cells to form a long tube. Critically, this neural tube developes into the spinal cord, the end of the tube, (the neural crest mid-point) the brain, and cells along its length evolved into melanocytes and all of the endocrine glands: pineal, pituitary, adrenal, mast cells, hypothalamus, thyroid, parathyroid, pancrease and many other glands found in the stomach, intestines, lungs and intestinal track (Roost, 1969; Welborn, 1974, 1977). A.G.E. Pearse (1974, 1969) rediscovered the critical fact that a great majority of cells producing hormonal peptides along the APUD series (Amine precursor uptake decarboxylase) share its distinctive cytochemical and ultrastructural characteristics. Again, all cells producing hormones of this APUD cell series originated from the melanin-containing ectoderm. "The APUD cells derive their name from the initial letters of their first three and most important properties, namely: (1) a high content of Amine, (2) the capacity for Amine Precursor Uptake, and (3) the presence of Amino Acid Decarboxylase for the conversion of the amino acid precursors to amines." One must know that the amines involved are such classic chemicals as dopamine, norepinephrine, tryptamine, and epinephrine, all precursors whose end product of metabolism is melanin. Another, of the amines found in such cells is 5-HT, 5 hydroxytryptamine or serotonin. This amine is the precursor to melanin, a key hormone of the pineal gland.

Black Dot Melanocyte Doorway To The Temple

The melanocyte is a pigment cell, found in skin that produces the black pigment melanin, and skin color. Our skin is an organ that covers the entire body. Direct sunlight, initiates the production of melanin, or skin color. Then too, melanocytes, though found in the skin, originate embryologically from the neural crest, an early prefetal structure which later evolves into the brain, and later migrates into skin sites. Thus, the melanocyte is a modified nerve cell that in terms of structure will resemble a nerve cell in appearance with dendrite axon cellular shape. The melanocyte is an example of a nerve that conveys information through long distance blood hormone messengers as compared to short range nerve neurotransmitters that are so typical of electrical forms information transferred by the nerves (Pearse, 1973; Pathak; Blois, 1969; Filators, 1976; Schneider, 1975; Riley, 1972; Wassermann, 1974; Edelstein, 1971).

The melanocyte can release its hormone, melanin, by two different paths. One way is by direct injection of melanin into skin cells as they grow out of the deep dermis-skin layer and pass through the melanocyte containing layer on their way to the epidermis (surface of the skin). Another way is for white blood cells to engulf melanin particles in the skin and then return to the blood circulatory tree inside of the white cell, traveling throughout the body, capable of being deposited in countless sites, circulating melanin.

Black Dot Eye Retina Melanin, Doorway To The Temple

The inner lining of our two lateral eyes contain the retina, a structure that contains both rods and cones. Rods are sensory organ receptors that produce black and white vision by literally capturing light when it passes through the pupil and reaches the retina. The rod converts the light into a chemical message that is passed to the optic nerve at the center of the retina, which in turn relays the message to the brain for processing. Cones are sensory organs that produce color vision by capturing light and converting it into the chemical message which is also passed along to the optic nerve and then the brain. Critically, melanin is present throughout the retina in a layer just below the surface of the rod and cone containing retina, the pigmented layer of the retina. When light reaches the rod, it is captured by the rod visual pigment rhodopsin, then changes shape from the cis (chair-shape) to the trans (boat-shape) and thereby holding the light photon, and the rhodospin containing disc is then shed, falling into the deeper melanin pigment layer of the retina. In the pigmented layer of the retina, the light photon in transferred to melanin, transrhodopin, changes shape into cis, and then returns to the rod for new-light reception. The energized melanin then generates an electrical-chemical message that passes into the optic nerve and then the brain. It is believed the color vision produced by the retina is also dependent upon a similar relationship with retinal melanin. These melanin retinal chemical events take place in less than a small fraction of a second. All human eyes contain retinal melanin, without which, one would be permanently blind. Light, (vision) is literally born from darkness, melanin (Path, 1978; Nettleship, 1909; O'Donnell, 1978; Creel, 1978).

Black Dot Inner Ear Nucleus, Doorway to the Temple

Melanin is also present in the inner ear nucleus. It has been shown that melanin in the inner ear of the fetus helps to direct inner ear nerve growth such that the nerve's (retinogenic-clostrate) projections, from one ear to the ear on the opposite side, allow coordinated hearing and vision. However, it has been found that there are birth defects that lack inner ear melanin, human ocular albinism, sex-linked ocular albinism and autosomal recessively inherited ocular albinism. Donald Creel (1980) reports, "However, both types of ocular albinos have congenital reduced visual acuity (20/400-20/50) and hypopigmentation of the urea and pigmented epithelia of the iris, ciliary body, and retina. As a result, human albinos have a 20 degree blind spot in their temporal fields and nystagmus, and constant fluttering of the eyes because poor nerve links induce poor circulation between both eyes and ears. Likewise, it has been shown that human albinos have hemisphere asymmetry in hearing sounds as a result of poor development of the abuducens nucleus in the brain. However, just as the melanin seed blue print in the ectoderm becomes the pattern from which brain spinal cord and endocrine glands evolve, so do eye and nerves depend upon inner ear melanin to outline the proper pattern and direction of growth (Peterson, 1980; Creel, 1978).

Black Dot Melanin, Memory Doorway To The Temple

The entrance into the African temple (which was symbolic of birth or creation into the human mind-body) was through a doorway bordered by two columns, two obelisks both topped by black pyramidions (Jochannan, 1980; Schwaller; Muller, 1964; Thompkins, 1971; James, 1976). These two obelisks at the entrance of the African temple symbolized the basic two opposites of nature - Y and B; male and female;

active, passive or positive, negative. Pathak (1972) reports, "Melanin pigmentation which follows exposure of skin to solar radiation (sunlight) is known to involve two distinct photobiological processes.

The first is immediate pigment-darkening, tanning, or direct pigmentation. The second is described as new pigment formation, melanogenesis." In fact melanin is black because of its unique physical properties that allows it to be an excellent electrical conductor or semiconductor. **Melanin is black because it absorbs light, colors or energy** (Blois, 1969; Filators, 1976). In fact, melanin responds to a critical applied electrical field by changing it's conductivity. The response falls into two categories, threshold and memory switching. Threshold switching occurs when sample cycles from an off (low conductivity) moves to an on (high conductivity) state at a critical electrical field, and returns to the off state when the electrical field is removed. Memory switching, on the other hand refers to a sample which remains in the on state when the field is removed but can be restored to the off state by larger electrical fields or currents. Both threshold and pseudomemory switching have been reported in melanin. The memory state is reversible, destroyed by heating above 110 C^o, suggesting the existence of a true memory state (Filators, 1976). Black Dot, is the doorway to the collective unconscious, the doorway through which chaos, hierarchy of energies, God, macrocosm, passes through to become the individual human mind, (ptah macrososm). Another example of melanin's role in memory pool operation can be seen in the report that D.N.A. itself, a key biological blueprint for life has been found to be directly linked to melanin granules (Schneider, 1975).

Again, there is a growing body of biological research that shows how the collective unconscious is recorded in our minds. A portion of our minds is clearly linked to our brains. The human brain has systematically evolved from animal ancestors: primate, mammal, reptilian, amphibian, fish, one-celled organisms. Indeed, MacLean (1970) notes that the human brain cortex is the newest brain layer super-imposed on earlier mammalian and reptilian brain structures.

Importantly, at the moment of conception and for the first several days afterwards, all animal embryos look amazingly alike, with the human fetus passing through the earlier biological ancestrial forms of fish through mammals. And it is in the oldest layer of the brain, the brain stem, that the black nerve tracts are found. Forrest (1972, 1975) shows that defects in the black neuromelanin tract can sometimes bring out behavior that was once used by humanities' ancestors.   Thus, when we consider the biological features of melanin, it's memory storage and capacity, it's presence in old brain centers, increased brain pigmentation in more advanced biological species, and innumberable reports of persons with detailed memory images of ancient historical concepts; the evidence is indeed overwhelming.

Rapid Eye Movement (REM) sleep, is that phase of sleep in which neophytes dream, and more specifically they dream historical memory images that come from the collective unconscious memory banks in the brain stem, black neuromelanin (Amenta) nerve tract, and passes through the locus coeruleus doorway.

The Black Dot, all black neuromelanin (Amenta) brain nerve tract, headed by the locus coeruleus, with multiple upper brain connection is a critical path followed by unconscious memory images as they move upward to become conscious.   Hobson and McCarley have recently defined the brain as a dream state generator and have outlined the great upward and downward flow of memory images of the brain system.   In fact, infants at six months who were found to possess extreme rapid eye movements (R.E.M. storms) during sleep were found to have possible delay of neurodevelopment.   Moreover, the more one investigates the dream collective unconscious system, the more one is impressed by the systems multiple relationship to melanin.   The pineal hormone, mela-tonin, a brain hormone released at night that induces skin color formations, acts upon the dream system to increase the movement of sensory images from the brain stem to the cortex, unconscious to consciousness, memory readout.   Serotonin, is a pineal hormone released during daylight, that increases the flow of memory images from the centers of the brain (consciousness) to unconscious, memory stor-age (Becker, 1981). The eleventh pigmented nucleus, just below the locus coeruleus is called the substantia nigra (Black substance) and is so named because of its large pool of melanin (Oneda, 1969; Moses, 1966; Hiroswa, 1968). When there is depigmentation or loss of melanin, people who are afflicted, develop Parkinson's disease, a disease of impaired motor movement and thought. This illness is treated by giving patients L-dopa, a chemical that produces melanin and replaces the lost melanin in the substantia nigra. However, when increased melanin is given, patients frequently expressed an increased range of vivid dreams, range of vivid dreams, hallucinations, illusions, confusional psychosis (Moskovitz), reflecting flooding of conscious by a flow of upward memory images.

In fact the primary medications used to treat psychosis, an illness whereby people poorly translate unconscious memory images, are phenothiazines; medications that are believed to work by dopamine blockage (Maclean, 1970). Basically, stimulants and allucinogens, such as amphetamines, LSD, DMT, mescaline, all increase melatonin, dopamine and melanin. Whereas, tranquilizers such as phenobarbital, decrease melatonin, dopamine and melanin formation. Furthermore melatonin (the pineal hormone that increases melanin when given to normal people) has been shown to increase feelings of tranquility and dream states in persons able to translate unconscious memory images. However, a person who was stable but with a prior history of psychosis or depression, when given melatonin, expressed within 24 hours a return of hallucinations of depression (Carman, 1976). Then too, the locus coerleus has been shown to contain and have very strong links to the system of naturally occurring opiates and opiod peptides. These are naturally occurring hormones that can induce strong feeling states that can guide and direct consciousness (Pepper, 1972).

Black Dot Melanin, Collective Unconscious Doorway To The Temple

The locus coeruleus is literally a brain doorway to the collective unconscious. It is a critical brain center that, when activated, will begin R.E.M. sleep, that phase of sleep in which we can recall dreams, the actual review of images from the collective unconscious (Hobson, 1977; Olswezski, 1954; Scherer, 1939; Jouvet and Delmorme, 1965; Huang, 1975; Kobayahi, 1975; Redmond, 1976; Moses, 1966; Van Woert, 1967). The brain dreams continuously and is constantly sending unconscious memory images from deeper mind-brain levels up to the cortex for possible conscious expression. However, in the uninitiated or neophyte student, who is ignorant of how to translate ancient African memories, may occassionally become conscious or aware of such images only in the R.E.M. phase of "dream" sleep during the night, and they may occasionally experience intuitive flashes during the day or night. Mental slaves, trained to remain ignorant of their own historical Africanity, remain fixed at this neophyte level. According to the great leader, the Honorable Elijah Muhammad, many Africans are mentally dead, unaware of how to use their own mind, unaware of the infinte power of their mind; that is far superior to any man-made computer.

Diverse physiological correlations of anxiety and fear led Cannon (1927) to suggest that they are mediated by the sympathetic nervous system. Maclean (1949), proposing his theory of the limbic system as the central mediator of emotion, transformed the anatomic site to the mid-brain. More recently, the locus coeruleus, a small streak of cells located in the dorsolateral tegmentum of the pons, has been proposed as another important mediator of anxiety (Redmond, 1974). All of these structures are phylogentically ancient, suggesting that anxiety itself evolved with man's earliest vertebrate ancestors. Experiments suggest a possible continuum of cautionary or inhibitory functions by this small nucleus in which the middle or normal range of function (vigilance, caution, prudence, watchfullness, attentiveness) would have evolutionary advantages, insuring that threats were respected, and where possible, prevented. Whereas excessive or maximum locus coeruleus function would have the disadvantages of terror, panic, fear, anxiety, dread and alarm. Minimum locus coerleus function would have the disadvantages of inattentiveness, distractability, impulsivity, carelessness, recklessness and fearlessness (Redmond, 1974; A Legacy of Evolution, 1981). An excellent example of Black Dot ancient memory that was pulled from the collective unconscious memory bank presented in a dream, and associated with fear and panic, was reported by the European psychiatrist C.G. Jung (1970).

"The dreamer receives a letter from an unknown woman. She writes that she has pain in the uterus. A drawing is attached to the letter, looking roughly like this:

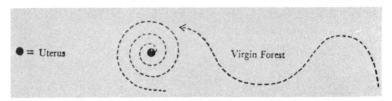

● = Uterus   Virgin Forest

Fig. 1 Uraeus, vol. 2.

In the virgin forest there are swarms of monkeys. Then a panorama of white glaciers opens up. Jung interpreted this dream, "The uterus is the center, the life giving vessel (vas). The serpentine line leading to the vessel is analogous to the healing serpent of Aesculapius (Medicina). It is also analogous to the Tantric symbol of Shiva Bindu, the creative latent god without expression in space who, in the form of a point or lingam, is encircled three and a half times by the kundalini (Uraeus) serpent with the virgin forest we meet the ape motif again. The present dream ends with the panorama of white 'glaciers', reminding the dreamer of earlier dreams of which he beheld the Milky Way and was having a conversation about immortality."

First, the dream and interpretation yield great supportive evidence to the universal symbol Black Dot, and its vast history even in European literature. Regarding Black Dot, the vessel, uterus or vas, Jung reported,

> "The center of the mandala is sometimes referred to in al-chemical literature as the vas. It corresponds to the salyx of the indian lotus, seat and birthplace of the gods. This is called the padma, a term that denotes femininity and corresponds to the yoni. In alchemy the vas is often taken as the uterus where the 'child' is gestated. In the *Litany of Loreto*, Mary is spoken of three times as the vas (Vas spirituale, Honorable and insigne devotions) and in medieval poetry she is called the 'flower of the sea', which shelters the Christ."

Second, Jung's oldest references for interpreting the dream was the Greek healing serpent Aesculapius and Indian kundalini serpent. The kundalini serpent, or Uraeus was shown to be a creative energy that passed through the Black Dot, uterus, doorway to life. By reference to our earlier discussion we can summarize that both the Greek and Indian references to the Black Dot, serpent relationship were taken from even earlier African scientists who predated both civilizations. Third, by not being aware of his own ancient African source, Jung was unable to translate the glacier and swarm of monkeys depicted in the dreams. He lacked an African consciousness that would have assisted his patient in accepting her own collective unconscious memory bank. To this end, she would have known that her European ancestors, who were Africans, migrated from Africa to European forests and then underwent various changes in an attempt to adapt to glacial conditions. For the patient to continue the individuation process, meant that the she would have to retrieve lost ancient African knowledge. To accept that part of herself, the dreamer had to accept her historical black self rather than distort and reject swarms of ancient Black ancestors as swarms of monkeys. Last, the dream took place because of the dreamer's intact Black born nerve tracts and nerve hormones, the indelible biological record of humanity's common African roots.

"The entrance to the Great Pyramid (Amenta, unconsious mind) was concealed by a movable flagstone that turned on a pivot, which none but the initiated could detect. Thus, Horus (inner vision) was the door in darkness, the way portrayed for the manas in death (transformation). Here is the mystery: How to enter where there is no door and the way is all unknown? It is explained to the manas how Divine assistance is to be obtained. When the strains of life on earth are effaced, strength is given, forging the entrance where there is no door and in that power the manas penetrate with, or, as the god." It was through the use of the Ten Virtues, Negative Confessions, and Seven Liberal Arts (King, 1978; James, 1976) that the heart was developed, the core of the emotional finger that pulls knowledge from the collective unconsious. A strong heart will yield a strong character of personality and well-tuned emotional radar. Consider and start daily use of the Ten Virtues; two of which are Courage-freedom from resentment; and Efficiency-preparation for initiation at all times. Black Dot is an ancient African symbol for blackness, the seed and archetype of all humanity. Black Dot is the hidden doorway to the collective unconscious, ancestral memory bank for all. Black Dot represents the African origin of all humanity; for all Europeans, Latinos, and Asians came from the same African ancestrial parents. Humanity may differ with variations of color (skin melanin) but we are all rooted in neuromelanin, black hormone blackness.

Today's reborn Black Master's must accept their Blackness, and be inspired to create genius levels, beauty, and rest upon and even surpass the pyramids. Uraeus is a symbol of the transforming energy of the soul. Black Dot defines the hidden doorway through which the transforming soul energy of Uraeus passes.

Chapter Three

BLACK DOT......BLACK SEED
Archetype of Humanity III

T he pineal gland or Eye of Horus is an excellent example of the ancient African study of biological blackness and states of consiousness. Pharoah Tut-ankh-Amun was an African King of the 19th dynasty of Ta-Merry Egypt who died in 1349 B.C. or more that 3,333 years ago. At the time of his death he was buried in a tomb filled with jewels, shrines statues and household goods. It was King Tut's tomb that has been publically acknowledged as being the most complete tomb of an Egyptian Pharoah that has ever been discovered. Of the many structures found in the tomb over fifty years ago there, is one shrine, which in graphic pictorial form, clearly displays the ancient African knowledge of the relationship of the Pineal Gland to sunlight, darkness and states of consciousness. This displayed a fact well known to ancient African scholars and priests more than 3,333 years before its discovery by European-African scholars in the late 1950's (Leek, 1972; Jochannan, 1978; Lamy, 1981; West, 1979; Gilbert, 1976; Romer, 1981; Piankoff, 1977).

Pharoah Tut-ankh-Amun's mummy was found inside the innermost coffin enclosed within two successive coffins. The three coffins were found inside of a quartzite sarcophagus. These four coffins were enclosed within four successive large box-like shrines. The surface of each of the four shrines was covered with elaborate tableaus. On the exterior right panel of shrine II in the left upper corner first register is a group of seven figures, and upright cobra, and six upright mummiform figures. A cobra projects rays of light onto the forehead of the first mummiform figure. The second and third figures receive light on their foreheads from a star above their heads. The four remaining figures have stars above their heads which pass a flow of light between the stars. Alexander Piankoff (1977) partially translated this register of figures and other representations on the right and left panels as "unique", though certain figures are similar to those in the tombs of Ramses VI and Ramses IX. Here they are accompanied by inscriptions in enigmatic script, where every current sign is replaced by another. The representations on both panels are extracts from an unknown cosmological composition dealing with the creation and the refilling of the solar disk with fire during the night. Here, in the region of death (underworld, Amenta, unconsious, Blackness) the sun passes through, bodies of gods who reside there. Their bodies remain in the dark (underworld, Amenta, unconsious, Blackness) while their souls, power, and essence, follow the sun in his journey. In other words, in the region of death the sun collects new energy for his rebirth in the morning (King, 1985, 1982; Hobson, 1971).

Regarding the seven figures of the right panel and upper left register, Piankoff has translated, "Above the representation is an enigmatic inscription: These gods are like this: the rays of Re (sun) enter their bodies. He calls their souls. It is indeed they who enter after the souls....the names of divinities: The cobra: The Rearer, first figure of the underworld; second figure: The Praiser; third figure: Opener; Fourth figure: Fine Stuff; fifth figure: The Incomplete One; sixth figure: The Weak One."   Thus, in this inscription there is reference to eight divinities, Re, the sun, the cobra, and six mummiform figures. It is important to note that the cobra is named the rearer, and on one symbolic level represents the snake shaped spinal column that holds the human body upright atop which rests the head containing the pituitary gland and the pineal gland. Two of the six mummiform figures receive the light of the sun, Re, directly into the forehead location of the pineal gland. Critically, the pineal release of hormones is determined by the presence of either sunlight or darkness (King, 1978; Wurtman, 1977; Quay, 1974). During sunlight the pineal releases into the blood stream the hormone serotonin. Whereas, during darkness the pineal releases into the blood stream the hormone melatonin. Serotonin is a memory storage hormone, it increases the flow of memories from the cortex into the brainstem. Melatonin is a memory read out hormone that increases the flow of memories into the cortex. More importantly, melatonin initiates dreams or R.E.M. sleep by activating the locus coeruleus, Black

Dot, the 12th and uppermost in a chain of 12 deeply pigmented nucleii found in the brainstem (King, 1982; Hobson, 1974; Carman, 1976; Moskovitz, 1978; Jouvet, 1965; Olswezki, 1954; Bazelon, 1967; Feinchel, 1968; Marsden, 1961; Scherer, 1939). Dreams have long been considered by many to be a royal road to the unconscious, making visible the soul, spirit, body and mind of various realms of consciousness. Thus, the pineal gland which was named by ancient Africans as the Eye of Horus is the eye of inner vision, that form of vision or consciousness that was the very goal of an entire educational process of the ancient Africans of Ta-Merry. George James (1976) said, "The Egyptian Mystery System had three grades of students (1) The Mortals, i.e., probationary students who were being instructed, but who had not yet experienced the inner vision, (2) The Intelligences, i.e., those who had attained the inner vision, and had received mind or nous, and (3) The Creators or Sons of Light, i.e., those who had attained true spiritual consciousness."

Additional proof of the ancient Egyptian knowledge of the anatomy and physiology of the pineal comes from a historical review of the study of the pineal gland. Modern science has deemed the Greek anatomist Herophilos (325-280 B.C.) as the first one to discover the pineal gland and to locate its primary site of action to be the brain ventricular system (Reiter, 1981). Yet, upon viewing pictures of the unwrapping of Pharoah Tut-ankh-Amun's head by Carter and Derry (Leek, 1972), in the 1920's there was found a golden bird that laid across the top of the crown of the head with outstretched wings covering the front of the head and the body of the bird along the center of the head. This may have been a symbolic statement of the actual African knowledge of the location of the soul being in the brain's ventricular system because the shape of the bird closely resembles the top-view appearance of the ventricular system. The lateral ventricles are similar to the outstretched wings and the bird's body is similar to the third and fourth ventricles (King, 1985; Feinchel, 1968; James, 1976). The pineal gland is located at the posterior end of the third ventricle and the pituitary gland, the hypthalamus anterior end of the third ventricle. The third ventricle has long been held to be the "vault of initiation." The perfectly clear fluid of the third ventricle has been named the "dew", the fluid that crystallizes spirit or light as it decends from the heavens to the earth (Hall, 1972). Modern science has now rediscovered that though the pineal hormones, serototonin and melatonin, are released into the blood.   In the case of melatonin it is found in the brain ventricular system fluid, cerebro-spinal fluid in concentrations that are 13 times greater than that found in the blood (Mess, 1975).   The cerebro-spinal fluid is produced within the brain ventricular system and flows throughout the inner ventricular chambers of the brain and leaves the brain near its base and then flows over the entire surface of the brain and the spinal column.   Modern science has now come to see that many important hormones produced in many sites throughout the body are found within fluid and travel in it much like a vast freeway to activate many receptor sites along the walls of the various chambers of the brain's internal ventricular system (Barr, 1982).

The notion of the bird representing the soul is indeed and old African concept.   A human-headed bird, Ba, was used by ancient Egyptians to represent the soul.   Whereas, the Benu bird or stork was used by these Africans to represent the spirit (Lamy, 1981).   Thus, to find the symbolic soul-spirit bird placed atop Pharoah Tut-ankh-Amun's head at death 1,000 years before the birth of Herophilos, shows a clear error in the Greek claim that Herophilos discovered the pineal and defined the soul to be in the brain ventricular system.   Furthermore, the ancient Egyptians built their temples as replicas of the human body.   They knew that the same powers present in the universe, macrocosm, were present in man, microcosm.   Thus, they painted the ceilings of their temples blue to represent the starry heavens (James, 1976).   In Pharoah Tut-ankh-Amun's tomb was found a statue of the god Ptah, who represented the mind or Memphite Cosmology hill emerging out of the primeval waters of Nun (space, great lakes region of Africa, blood, cerebro-spinal fluid). The (Shabaka) (Memphite) Cosmology held that the sun, Atum, sat atop the hill.   This statue of Ptah has the crown of the head painted blue to represent that there is in the crown of the heads all human organs that link them to the sun and stars of the blue heavens (the pineal gland which releases different hormones in response to sunlight and darkness).

Concerning the translation of the exterior right panel, first top register of the second shrine of Tut-ankh-Amen a new interpretation has been offered by Egyptologist, Rkhty Wimby.   This is a critical interpretation because of the translator's use of an Afrocentric perspective and thorough research skills.   Rkhty Wimby noted, "This inscription is written in a special script or code, which was then perhaps known to the

Priest/Scribes. The language therein is highly symbolic/theological in nature. This code was first discerned by Champollion, who had determined the value of many of the signs. Piankoff (1977), benefiting from the work of others, made an admirable attempt at translating. Yet he seems not to have recognized the value of all signs. I have been able to determine the value of two signs myself.

The script is a code, using common signs having other than their ususal value. Furthermore determinatives were not written, determinatives are pictures which occur on the end of words. Out of the many meanings for any given root, in our code there is nothing to indicate what meaning is intended. One need have some foreknowledge of what the inscription is about (the pictoral representations help). Another problem is that the meaning of many words, in this script, is unknown and it is not always clear where one word ends and the next begins. Finally, these special inscriptions are full of word play of different kinds, which are additional elements of great significance. This is why I have included in the notes different meanings for certain word-roots not to miss possible word play.

The translation offered by Rkhty Wimby is as follows:

(Exterior Right Panel - Shrine of Tut-ankh-amen, First
Top register.)

These are in this condition
Rays of light enter their bodies;
He calls forth their Bas
They (Rays) penetrate them,
So that they may accompany them.

Serpent
1) The Morning
2) The Praiser
3) The Opener
4) The Keres
5) The Incomplete One
6) The Corruptible Flesh

These Neters are in this condition.
Their heads -

1) Head of Horus
2) Face of Horus
3) Neck of Horus
4) 133 - tissue of Horus
5) (Inner ?) Eye
6) The Doorway

These Neters are in this condition.
Their Bas coil,
so that their (Bodies) may become Ba-like.
The Herret Serpent of Ra burns,
because of their Bas.
They (Rays) penetrate them,
so that they may ascend

(Behind each serpent is its name mhm "The Coiled One")
Cat
1) Submerged One
2) ?
3) Ejaculator
4) Innundator
5) Babe in Swaddling Cloth
6) The Morning Bark of Ra
You will be among the Neters. You will not be distinguished from them
- Wsir, True of Voice - Vindicated.

Another central African philosophical concept that clearly supports the evidence that the pineal gland was first discovered by Africans is taken from the second shrine of Pharoah Tut-ankh-Amun's tomb that depicts stars passing rays of light into the mid-forehead pineal gland anatomical site. Not only does this define the pineal gland relationship to sunlight, this also illustrates the ancient African concept of the "third eye" or Eye of Heru (Horus). The Eye of Horus was said to have been given to Horus, son of Isis and Osiris, to replace a shattered left eye that had been damaged by evil Seth. It was the god Thoth, god of magic and writing, that gave Horus this new eye (Lamy, 1981). Symbolically, Horus represents the union of opposites, male and female, just as the pineal gland is found in the exact mid-line of the brain between the masculine left cortical hemisphere and feminine right cortical hemisphere. It has been said by authors that the pineal actually greatly increases in it's hormone output and synchronization with other glands in the brain and along the spinal column axis as psychic energy is developed and raised to progressively higher levels along the spinal column (Mtengwa, 1982) For just as Horus had to overcome an external evil Seth, who had dismembered his father Osiris, so too must each human overcome their own internal evil and misconceptions. Yet, the concept of a third eye is linked to a phylogenetic fact that in lower life forms the pineal gland was an actual third eye that did receive light and functioned as an eye in some lizards and reptiles. In higher vertebrates and in humans the pineal gland withdrew into the interior of the brain, retained its connection to sunlight and darkness but instead of producing visual images, it now released hormonal signals that unlocked internal memory banks of visual and other sensory images i.e., dreams and higher states of consciousness (King, 1979; Quay, 1974). This is the physiological basis of the ancient African Statement that, of the three grades of students, those at the intelligence level of student had received mind or nous and developed inner vision, activated pineal gland, release of higher hormone output of the dream activating hormone, melatonin. Furthermore, the next and highest grade of student, sons of light, were said to not only have mind and innervision but also unity with light, a clear reference to even more sophisticated relationships between personal behavior, psychological-physiological transformation, and pineal gland links to light in a multitude of ways (sunlight, starlight, moonlight, biological aural light).

The very dates of Herophilos lifetime (325-280 B.C.) places him at a time when the library of Alexandria was first opened by the Greeks following their overthrow of the short term Persian rulers of Egypt (525-332 B.C.). Alexandria was a northern coastal city of Egypt that already had a Royal Library prior to the Persian and Greek invasions of Egypt. Herophilos did his major anatomical studies at the later Greek controlled library of Alexandria. George James (1954) has written, "Before the time of Psammitichus, the Greeks were not allowed to go beyond the coast of Lower Egypt but during the reign of King Amasis 670 B.C., those conditions were modified. For the first time in Egyptian history Ionians and Carians were employed as mercenaries in the Egyptian army. In addition to these changes, King Amasis removed the restrictions against the Greeks and permitted them to enter Egypt and settle in Naucratis. The immigration of the Greeks to Egypt, for the purpose of education, began as a result of the Persian invasion (525 B.C.) and continued until the Greeks gained possession of that land and access to the Royal Library, through the conquest of Alexander the Great (332 B.C.). Alexandria was converted into a Greek city, a centre of research (University and Library of Alexandria) and the capital of the newly created Greek empire, under the rule of the Ptolemies. Any invading army would first loot the Royal Library of Alexandria and then would turn their attention to the Memeptheion at Thebes (Grand Lodge of Luxor, center of the world-wide African University system, The Mystery System). They would also invade the cities of Memphis and Heliopolis and likewise loot their libraries and temples. The Greeks (i.e., Alexander the Great, Aristotle's school and the succeeding Ptolemies) converted the Royal Library of Alexandria into a research centre by transfering Aristotle's school and pupils from Athens to this great Egyptian Library, and therefore the students who studied there received instruction from Egyptian priests and teachers, until they died out. For the next 700 years, science had its chief abiding place." Thus, Greek scholars such as Herophilos who were present at the opening of the Greek controlled Library of Alexandria did not first discover the pineal gland, but read of the pineal gland from pre-existing African books and were taught by existing African scholars. The multiple references to the pineal gland found in the tomb of Pharoah Tut-ankh-Amun, buried 1,000 years before the time of Herophilos and the Greek invasion, certainly bear this point out in abundant detail.

The Ancient African Study of States of Consciousness, Black Dot

Naim Akbar (1985) has written, "Despite the impressive technologi-cal advancement of modern Western man relative to his own history, he ranks far behind the Ancient African people of KMT (Egypt) both technologically and spiritually. Part of the reason for this mental de-evolution is the limited conception of human potential that one finds in Western science." Western man's limitation is a disaster for his captives, who are the descendants of the people of Ancient Kemet. The possible advancement of Western man and the redemption of "renaissance" of African man is contingent upon rediscovering those concepts of human development which inspired the ascension of the people of Ancient Africa. Euro-American psychology approached its duty of man; an orientation to the study of the human being results in what Schwaller de Lubicz (1978) calls "research without illumination." This distortion resulted in two rather serious problems for the Western scholar; one problem was his fear of the matriarchy and the need to inferiorize women. The other problem affecting the European distortion of mental science was a pervasive racism which has permeated the interaction of Europeans with African people and African knowledge. As Diop (1967) has pointed out: "the common denominator which characterizes the mindset of the Egyptologists (as repeated in their various theses about Africa) is their seeming desperate necessity and unrelenting attempt to refute ancient Africa's Blackness. The fundametal error of dichotomizing man's make-up into mind and body and eliminating the spirit altogether was done in the glory of the material or the physical. Therefore, the spiritual or non-material world was relegated to the practitioners of the 'Dark Sciences' and essentially given to the dark races, but not without degrading such involvement as superstitious, primitive (in the sense of uncivilized) and unscientific (i.e., ignorant). On the other hand, the physical and material was the source of thought, action, intellect and science. Therefore, the material was superior and its practitioners (the Aryan races) were a superior people." Akbar maintains that ancient Africans paid extraordinary attention to higher states of consciousness present in man more so than the physical level of consciousness. This was the emphasis of the higher mind (Ka), soul (Ba), and spirit (Khu). Akbar said, "Man was viewed as the fundamental metaphor for all higher truth. The gods (neters) and most importantly the Pharoah, all stood as symbols of profound truth. So, clearly the understanding of man (mind) was viewed as paramount in the science, the wisdom and the theology of Ancient Egypt. Schwaller de Lubicz (1967) describes the Egyptian view of man as a microcosm: Man is a microcosm in the sense of a tree in relation to a seed. Potentiality is the macrocosm, since it includes all the possibilities of the tree. The seed will develop these possibilities, however only if it receives correspond-ing energies from the earth and sky. Even more so, man who bears within him the total seed of the universe, including the seed of spiritual states can identify with the totality and obtain nourishment from it. The dictum now correctly identified with its source, of "Man Know Thyself", was the fundamental principle of the psychology of Kemet. George James, goes on to describe the Ancient Egyptian doctrine of self-knowledge by observing: Self Knowledge is the basis of all Knowledge. The mysteries required as a first step, the mastery of the passions, which made room for the occupation of unlimited powers. Hence as a second step, the neophyte was required to search within himself for the new powers which had taken possession of him. Schwaller de Lubicz (1967) observes that the universe is only consciousness from beginning to the end; the end being a return to its cause. This implies evolution of an innate conscious toward the psychological consciousness that is con-sciousness of the innate consciousness, the first step towards the liberated consciousness of physical contingencies.

Akbar has outlined several critical issues that are relevant to the Ancient African study of states of consciousness--the genetic descen-dants of Ancient Egyptians in the modern world diaspora of North America, South America, and the West Indies; Aryan materialism, Aryan rejection of matriarchy and Blackness, higher levels of conscious-ness and innate consciousness. Without question these are all extremely important and interrelated concepts. One way of analysis is a historical one, where the issues unfold for us as they unfolded in the history of humanity. Solon (638-559 B.C.), a Greek Athenian statesman who framed the democratic laws of Athens after visiting Egypt, has his voyage recorded by Plato (Sauneron, 1969; Plato, Timeus): "Solon said that the people of Sais received him very well, and in interrogating the priests wisest in these matters on the antiquities, he stated that no one among the Greeks, and he above all, knew a single word of these questions. One day, to induce the Egyptian priests to expound on the antiquities, he began to relate all the most ancient things we know: Phoconeus, said to be the first mane, Niobe, the Flood of Deucalion and Pyrrha, with everything he had been about it. He gave the geneology of all their descendants; he tried, by calculating the years to determine the date of these events. But the oldest one among the Egyptian priests exclaimed: "Solon, Solon, you Greeks are always children, there are no old men in Greece!" "What are you trying to say?" asked Solon. "You are young in spirit", replied the priest, "for you possess no truly antique tradition, no notion gray with time". And the old priest continued his proof: permanent catastrophes trouble the surface of the globe, mix or change the races, destroying one civilization to replace it with another; the last, far from absorbing the intellectual and scientific heritage of the one preceding it, picks up at the beginning and has to traverse again the entire lost road.

Manetho, the last publicly known high priest of ancient Egypt, who was made by the Greeks to compose a list of rulers of Egypt, gave a somewhat different series of dates to the "pre-history" of Egypt: 15,150 years of divine dynasties and 9,777 to all the kings who ruled before Menes for a total of 24,927 years. Diop (1982) defined the protohistoric figure of Tera-Neter as a negro nobleman of the Amous race as the first inhabitants of Egypt. Importantly, the Amous race appear to be a race of small statured people, similar to the small size people, Twa, who as Homo Erectus, were the first human beings to migrate outside of Africa to inhabit every continent on earth. Dr. Ben Jochannan (1981) lists three periods of 100,000 years each for a total of 300,000 years, Sebellian periods I, II, and III, as periods of human habitation before "historical" or dynastic Egypt. Sterling Means (1945) made reference to the Ethiopians who orally record themselves as the original inhabitants of Egypt, people who settled at a distant time so remote that Egypt was largely marsh and swamp land. It is most critical to note that Egypt in this sense may have been Lower Egypt of the North Delta region, geologically this is a very plastic region constantly in change as a result of top soil deposition by the Nile and the periodic rise and fall of the Mediterranean Sea Level in relationship to cyclical ice ages. Whereas, Upper Egypt was in very ancient times a part of Ethiopia. As George James noted, "Thebes in its prime occupied a large area of both sides of the Nile. This city was the centre of a great commercial nation of Upper Egypt." Thus, the old Egyptian priest with whom Solon held audience was ever so correct to acknowledge hundreds of thousands of years of high cultures, some as advanced if not more so than the present day. "But Egypt, through its geographical and climatic characteristics avoids this most general rule: For in Egypt, in any case, the waters do not rush from the mountain heights but seem, on the contrary, to spring from the earth. That is why, thus spared, it is said that here are preserved the oldest traditions. Thus, there is nothing beautiful or great nor remarkable done, be it in your country, or here in another country known to us, which has not long since been consigned to writing and preserved in our temples."

Black Dot, Daath, and Racial Perceptions of the Historical Desert

It is important to note that the Egyptian priest acknowledged the importance of geology and weather in determining styles of human culture, and the "fixed" psychological climate of the then inhabitants of Greece. He also acknowledge that the Greeks, "always being children", possessed greater difficulty in appreciating ancient events externally and internally. He also acknowledged the human tendency to suffer traumatic psychological scars when undergoing cultural change in response to geological catastrophe that made it difficult to build upon the achievements of ones ancestors and often resulted in laborious repetitions of discovery and inventions that had long preceded the "new culture." This latter issue is totally contrary to present notions of historical evolution that position the current western world as the progressive step by step evolutionary historical advancement of human culture from a much less advanced primitive past to a most advanced Aryan or European-African present. Apparently, the continued coverup of high cultures and great scientific achievements of African cultures prior to Aryan cultures is partially conscious and unconscious. From a conscious perspective this is done to exact blind obedience from mentally enslaved Africans who are forced to see their European-African masters as gods and themselves as out classed. By doing so, Africans view the products of their own minds as worthless and do little to develop such ideas. Then too, if such ideas are developed the mental slave African will not have the conviction to protect such ideas from theft. Rather they will do what the master says or sadly give away their mental products with minimal compensation and little concern for the consequential impact on their communities. They will not put their lives at risk in protecting their children.

From an unconscious perspective European-Africans have grave difficulty recalling memories of pre-Aryan high cultures because it reminds them of associated memories that shortly followed or where simultaneous with such cultures, the ice age conditions of Northern Eurasia. Closely allied with such memories are the memories of the psychological fall and change from African matriarchal agrarian societies to ice age Eurasian patriarchal nomadic societies. Even more so was the loss of pineal activation for many following pineal calcification and its resultant entrapment at the doorway to Daath.

In an article entitled, "Home of Man, Notes and Bibliography, The Cycles of Civilizations Black Gnostic Studies" (Black Gnostic Studies 1980), it is written, "Dr. Churchward has given the age of Original Primary Man as 2,000,000 years. From the Pygmy (Twa, Homo Erectus), evolution continued progressively into groups: 1) The Non-Totemic Group or Pre-Totemic people, 2) The Totemic people, 3) The Nilotic people, 4) The Stellar Mythos people. Afterwards the Stellar, Lunar and Solar Cult people followed and various exodes of these left Egypt. The Sun travels around its center once in every 25,920 years forming 'The One Great Year', and during that period the Northern Hemisphere is frozen down to about the 56th degree latitude part of the time. There is a great Autumn, great Winter and great Spring in the Sun's year, as in our year of 365 days. When Herodotus was in Egypt the Mystery Teachers of the heavens told him that during a certain length of time (39,000 years) the Sun, had four times deviated from its ordinary course, having twice set where it uniformly rises. This, however, had produced no alteration in the climate of Egypt; the fruits of the earth and the phenomena of the Nile was always the same, nor had any extraordinary or fatal diseases accrued" (Herodutus, Eutupes CXLII). No astronomer throughout the modern world has ever been able to explain this, nor have they taken into consideration the knowledge of the Wise Men of Egypt, except, probably Major-General Drayson. He, in his works corroborates the facts that were known to these old wise men although I do not think he mentions the Mystery Teachers. Thus, we have here an oral historical record of actual written records that were over 11,000 years old in an age that required advanced mathematics, geometry, physics, optics, climatology, geology, etc., on the part of ancient Africans to make and maintain such advance scientific records. And as the old Egyptian priest noted despite claims that modern science is the most advanced, the critical message of the African scientist, that weather is a constantly changing affair and so too with culture, today's world rather than being able to listen and build upon the achievements of ancestors will have to learn the same lessons all over again.

During the 9th dynasty, 3000 B.C., before the first Eurasian invasion of Egypt by the Hyksos a Pharoah passed on to his heir the following wisdom, according to Dr. Jacob Carruthers (1984), "Lo the miserable Asiatic, he is wretched because of the place he's in, short of water, bare of wood. It's paths are many and painful because of mountains. He does not dwell in one place. Food propels his legs. He fights since the time of Horus." Clearly such a reference points to early African knowledge of the psychological differences of the people emerging from post ice-age Eurasia, nomadic lifestyle, and war-like mentality.

Next, there are other written records that speak of ancient advanced African civilizations that have been lost to current-day European-African history. R.A. Schwaller de Lubicz (1982) has cited several historical documents that support the concept of the 36,000 year pre-dynastic history of Egypt. He cited the papyrus of the Turin, an ancient Egyptian papyrus now kept in a museum in the northern Italian city of Turin. This papyrus contains a complete list of the Pharoahs who reined over Upper and Lower Egypt from the first dynasty of Menes to the New Empire of the 18th Dynasty, including the duration of each reign. However, in the papyrus' first column that precedes the column containing Menes is a list of "pre-historical" rulers of Upper and Lower Egypt. These were the divine dynasties of gods and heroes that included a list of Neters that ruled for 23,000 years and included Ptah, Ra, Shu, Geb, Osiris, Seth, Thoth, Ma'at and Horus. Following the divine dynasties the Papyrus of Turin listed a series of mortal kings who ruled Egypt for 13,420 years before Menes, the venerables of Memphis, venerables of the North, and Shemsu-Hor or "Companions of Horus."

Sunlight, Ice Ages, Pineal Calcification & Racial Styles of Consciousness

The planet Earth has gone through multiple ice ages in the past 500,000 years. During the ice age period the Northern Hemisphere

(North America, Europe, Northern Asia) is frozen down to about the 56th degree of latitude (Black Gnostic Studies, 1980). Whereas, the Southern Hemisphere (Africa, South America, Southern Asia, Austrailia) receives increased rainfall during this same period. Ocean levels are also lower during ice ages such that the Mediterranean sea level falls and the water recedes from the Nile Delta, drying Delta marsh and swamp lands and extending the coast line of the Delta region northward. The last ice age, Warm glaciation, ended about 10,000 years ago. Cheikh Anta Diop (1985), has defined the emergence of Causcasoids and Mongoloids from pre-existing Black parents. The Grimaldi and Hottentot populations (Twa) present in pre-Warm ice age Europe, "The man born in Africa was necessarily dark-skinned due to the considerable force of ultraviolet radiation in the equatorial belt. As he moved toward the more temperate climates, this man gradually lost his pigmentation by the process of selection and adaptation. It is from this perspective that the appearance of Cro-Magon Man in Europe must be seen. In the Solutrean he is seen after 20,000 years of adaptation and transformation from the Grimaldi negroid where he was found and no pre-historical archeology has provided any other explanation for his appearance."

Bernard Campbell's book, *Humankind Emerging,* defined the physiological relationships that promoted changes in skin color as a result of African migrations to Europe and glacial cold cycles. When people settled permanently in regions with less sunlight and did not get enough vitamin D, pigment was no longer a protection but a drawback.

Vitamin D exists in four forms, Vitamin D1, 2, 3 and 4. Vitamin D1 and 2 are inactive forms of vitamin that circulate throughout the body in the blood stream (Holick, 1980; Beeson, 1968). As blood, containing Vitamin D passes through the dermal dermis layer of skin, light is often able to penetrate the upper epidermal layer of skin, and Vitamin D in the dermal blood containing level energizes and converts Vitamin D 3 and 4. Vitamin D3 and 4, while passing in blood in the intestinal lining is able to actively transport calcium across cell membranes from the intestinal lumen into the blood supply and whole body distribution. However, in ice-age Europe there was frequent cloud cover. Thick animal skin clothing, and a dark pigmented upper epidermis level caused inadequate amounts of sunlight to reach the deeper dermal layer in order to activate Vitamin D. These environmental factors resulted

in a reduced ability to retrieve calcium from dietary sources thereby de-
pleting body calcuim levels and consequently bone deformations (rickets) occurred.

There are at least three other glands and classes of hormones
involved in bone physiology in addition to Vitamin D: (1) parathyroid
gland that produces parapthyroid hormone, (2) thyroid parafollicular
cells that produce thyrocalcitonin hormone, and (3) pineal gland that
produces serotonin and melatonin. The Parathyroid hormone promotes skeletal homeostatasis, and calcium ion concentration in the
extracellular fluid. It pushes calcium into the bone for absorption and
incorporation of calcium in bone growth. Thyrocalcitonin does the
reverse. It pulls calcium out of the bone structure thereby raising the
calcium level in the extracellular fluid including blood levels of calcium
ion concentration. Interestingly, the pineal gland controls both the
parathyroid and thyrocalcitonin for in examples where the pineal gland
was removed in laboratory animal experimentation, pinealectomy resulted in hyperlasia of the parafollicular cells of the thyroid and
hypofunction of the parathyroid, all of which could be restored to
normal by the administration of the pineal hormone melatonin (Daramola, 1972).

There appears to exist an even more profound relationship of
calcium to the pineal gland. Calcium in the form of hydroxy appetite or
bone formation is found in the structure of the pineal gland, from small
particles the size of fine sand grains to large solid nuggets that are
actually visible upon physical inspection of the pineal post-mortem or
in skull x-rays (Pilling, 1977; Earle, 1965; Mable, 1974). When the pineal
gland is heavily infiltrated with large amounts of calcium (pineal
calcification), though remaining pineal tissue continues to manufacture
and release melatonin it does so in greatly reduced amounts. People
with a non-calcified pineal gland will usually possess a blood serum level
of about 70 Ng. However, people with a calcified pineal gland will
experience a 50% decrease in blood serum levels such that they average
melatonin levels of about 35 Ng., (Pelham, 1973).

There are racial differences in pineal calcification that broadly
parallel the intensity of skin pigmentation. The darker the skin
pigmentation the lower the incidence of pineal calcification. Thus, adult
Black African populations in Africa and North America have recorded
pineal calcification incidence rates of 5-15% (Daramola, 1972; Adeloye,

1974). Whereas, European populations in Europe and North America experience pineal calcification incidence rates of 60%-80% in adult population (Naffzger, 1925; Dyke, 1930; Vastine, 1927). Asian populations in India, Japan and China experience pineal calcification incidence rates of 15-25%.

Thus, for African populations that remained in the ice-age Europe there was not only a decrease in skin pigmentation but also a decrease in pineal hormone output of the hormone melatonin. On a biological and physiological level this change played a profound contributory role in the change of consciousness from the spirit-focused matriarchal African to the material-focused patriarchal European-African. Perhaps with only 1/2 of the melatonin key to unlock the locus coeruleus doorway to neuromelanin all Black Amenta (inner vision), many European-Africans with pineal calcification had access to only surface levels of the unconsious thus, perpetually clunging to surface forms of things, such as materialism, their only real reality.

Naim Akbar's notion of the European-African rejection of ancient African spiritual concepts, as uncivilized, is correct, evidenced by the European-African Sigmund Freud's statement to C.G. Jung in the reference to the latter's interest in deeper levels of the unconscious. 'I can still recall vividly how Freud said to me, "My dear Jung, promise me never to abandon the sexual theory. That is the most essential thing of all. You see, we must make a dogma of it, unshakable bulwark. And promise me this one thing, my dear son, promise that you will go to church every Sunday." In some astonishment I asked him, "bulwark against what?" To which he replied, "Against the black tide of mud" and here he hesitated for a moment, then added, "of occultism" (Sulloway, 1979). Furthermore, Jung commented on Freud's attitudes at this time (1907-1910), "Above all, Freud's attitude toward the spirit seemed to me highly questionable. Wherever, in person or in a work of art, an expression of spirituality (in the intellectual, not the supernatural sense) came to light, he suspected it and insinuated that it was repressed sexuality. Anything that could not be directly interpreted as sexuality he referred to as "psychosexuality" (Sulloway, 1979; Jung, 1963).

C.G. Jung, another European-African psychiatrist, though more in touch with deeper levels of the unconscious, was still troubled as evidenced by his own reports,

I was not to recognize the real nature of this disturbance until some years later, when I stayed in tropical Africa. It had been, in fact, the first hint of 'going back under the skin', a spiritual peril which threatens the uprooted European in Africa today to an extent not fully appreciated. "On a jagged rock above us a slim, brownish-black figure stood motionless, leaning on a sling spear, looking down at the train. I was enchanted by this sight, it was a picture of something utterly alien and outside my experience, but on the other hand a most intent sentiment, deja vu. I had the feeling that I had already experienced this moment and had always known this world was separated from us only by distance and time. It was as if I were at this moment returning to the land of my youth, and as if I knew that dark-skinned man who had been waiting for me for five thousand years. The feeling tone of this curious experience accompanied me throughout my whole journey through savage Africa. I can recall only one other such recognition of the immemorially known. "Where danger is, there is salvation also". These words of Holderin often came to my mind in such situations. The salvation lies in our ability to bring the unconscious urges to consciousness. At the sight of the solitary dark hunter, I knew only that his world had been mine for countless millenia.

Thus, the going black under the skin, was for C.G. Jung, acknowledgement of his Black African ancestry and memories of African ancestral heritage contained within deeper levels of his collective unconscious.

Both of these European-African psychiatrists were major figures who led the movement and rediscovery of the unconscious (Amenta) in the 20th century. Yet, if these notable men experienced conflict in coming to terms with their African ancestral memories then we can expect the same denial from European-Africans, who are less aware of the operation of the unconscious. It is interesting to note that Freud lumped together mud and spirituality. Whereas, Jung linked spirituality with ancestral African memories. Freud's black mud referred to memories of his Black African ancestors which he rejected as something unclean and beneath his feet, i.e. underworld. Jung embraced the concept of the collective unconscious and ancestral memories, but was similarly stuck as indicated by his reference to his fear of a spiritual peril of going black underneath the skin. Since he considered his skin to be white he clearly fought the awareness that his insides were indeed Black. Yet, it is to Freud's credit that one year before his death in 1939 (he knew that he was dying of cancer of the jaw, and no longer held by the material relationships of politics, money power, and property) he wrote in his book, *Moses and Monethism.* "A new complication arises, however, when we become aware that what probably exists in the mental life of the individual is not only what he experiences, but also what he brought with him at birth, fragments of phylogenetic origin, and archaic heritage. On second thought I must admit that I have argued as if there were no question that there exists an inheritance of memory-traces of what our forefathers experienced, quite independent of direct communication and the influence of education by example. When I speak of an old tradition still alive in people, of the formation of a national character, it is such an inherited tradition, and not one carried by word of mouth, what I have in mind. Or at least I did not distinguish between the two, and I was not clear about what a bold step I took by neglecting this difference." Critically, at this point in Freud's life, when he embraced, the concept of archaic or ancestral memories he also approached his African ancestry by defining that Moses was an Egyptian.

Freud also asked the questions of what determines how an experience in one's external world enters into the ancestral memory bank and how the movement of ancestral memory moves from the ancestral bank into a person's conscious mind. Freud's (1939) reply, "...it happens when the experience is important enough, or is repeated often enough, or is of both cases. The awakening, however, of the memory traced through a recent real repetition of the event is certainly the decisive importance."

These issues are important in understanding present day relationships between African-Africans and European-Africans. Francis Cress Welsing (1970), author of *The Cress Theory of Color Confrontation and Racism (White Supremacy),* has said of such relationships, "The theory of Color-Confrontation states that the white or color deficient Europeans responded psychologically with a profound sense of numerical in-inadequacy and color inferiority upon their confrontations with a massive majority of the world's people all of whom possessed varying degrees of color producing capacity. This psychological reponse, be it described as conscious or unconscious, was one of deeply sensed inadequacy that struck a blow at the most fundamental part of their being, their external appearance.

As might be anticipated in terms of modern psychological theories, an uncontrollable sense of hostility and aggression developed, and continued to manifest throughout the entire historical epoch of mass confrontations of whites with people of color. The initial defensive hostility and aggression came from whites, and is recorded in innumerable diaries, journals and books written by whites. It is a matter of record, also, that only after long periods of great abuse have "non-whites" responded defensively with any form of counter-attack. This phenomenal psychological reaction of whites has been directed towards all people with the capacity to produce melanin skin pigments. However, the most profound aggressions have been directed towards Black, "non-white" peoples who have the greatest color potential and therefore are the most envied and the most feared in genetic competition.

The sense of numerical inadequacy and genetic color inferiority led to a number of interesting although devastating to all "non-white" peoples, psychological defensive mechanisms. The initial psychological defensive manuever was the "repression" of the initially felt thought or sense of inadequacy-being without color and, of secondary importance, being in deficient numbers, both of which were apparently painful awareness. This primary ego defense repression, was then reinforced by a host of other defensive mechanisms. One of the most important was a "reaction formation" response whose aim was to convert (at the psychological level) something that was desired and envied (skin color) but which was wholly unattainable, into something that is discredited and despised. The whites, desiring to have skin color but not being able to achieve this end on their own, said in effect, consciously or unconsciously, that skin color was disgusting to them and began attributing negative qualities to color and especially to the most intense state of skin color-Blackness.

Another psychological defense manuever utilized by whites is "projection." Feeling extreme hostility and hate towards "non-whites", whites began the pattern of stating that "non-whites" or people with skin color, hated them. In many instances, this mechanism has served to mitigate the guilt whites occasionally feel for constantly feeling the need to aggress against Black and other "non-white" peoples.

Here, we must again return to the great issues raised by the Ancient Egyptian priest in his statements to the Greek Solon. The priest claimed that the Greeks were *always children,* young in spirit, possessing no true antique tradition. Next the priest pointed to the ancient Egyptian records and their multiple references to the rise and fall of other civilizations in response to geological catastrophes, that troubled the surface of the globe and resulted in a strange effect upon human states of consciousness. The priest noted that the new culture that followed the preceeding one did not pick up where the other left off but had to traverse again the entire lost road. This was an ancient African observation and definition of a condition that was later renamed by modern western science as Traumatic Neurosis or Post-Traumatic Stress Syndrome. Post-Traumatic Stress Syndrome is characterized by (1) existence of a recognizable stressor that would evoke significant symptoms of distress in almost everyone, (2) re-experiencing the trauma, (3) numbing of responsiveness to or reduced with the external world, and (4) symptoms that were present before the trauma.

The re-experiencing of trauma may take place in several events. One form is the recurrent and intrusive recollections of the event. This is extremely important for at times it can take on psychotic proportions in terms of the degree of distortion, fragmentation and hallucination. It does this as a defensive manuever to shield against conscious awareness of the unconscious and to avoid reliving past trauma and its associated cluster of feelings experienced at the time of the trauma. Another form is recurrent dreams of the event. The last event of this category can be a sudden acting as if the traumatic event were reoccuring because of an association with an environmental stimulus.

Experience of numbing responsiveness to the external world, beginning after the trauma, can also have several forms; markedly diminished interest in one or more significant activities, feelings of detachment from others can be present, as well as, constriction or loss of the ability to feel empathy/sympathy for the feelings of others.

There may be symptoms present that were not present before the trauma, (1) hyper-alertness or exaggerated startle response (vague paranoia), (2) sleep disturbance (avoidance or recurrent dreams of the event), (3) guilt about surviving when others have not, or about behavior required for survival, (4) memory impairment or troubled concentration, (5) avoidance of activities that arouse recollections of the traumatic event, (6) intensification of symptoms by exposure to events that symbolize the traumatic event. The last two symptoms are of particular importance to those European-African and a few African-Africans that suffered pineal calcification. For the major event was not just the ice age in regards to skin color, Vitamin D and Calcium. The major traumatic event was pineal calcification and loss of spiritual consciousness. As a result of such trauma Europeans are often magnetically drawn to Africans who symbolize spiritual awareness with the expectation of regaining spirituality.

It is obvious that Ancient Africans had achieved an operative awareness of spiritual consciousness, as discussed earlier, in viewing objects from the tomb of Pharoah Tut-ankh-Amun. The African priest's claim that the Greeks were *always children* may suggest that some ancient Africans were well aware of the fragmented epistemology of the Greeks and their undeveloped spiritual consciousness. The Greeks were already suffering from pineal calcification that marked their "Fall from the Tower", the stone was placed on the Horus Doorway to Amenta. A strictly left brain approach to consciousness developed, damaging the ability to unify the two cerebral opposites, "The-intelli-gence-of-the-heart", a practice mastered by Africans for hundreds of years. The rigid left brain approach possibly prevented initiation for many into some phases of the African educational system, resulting in jealously towards those Africans who were able to gain access. Yet the central issue is that such a strictly logical perspective was a material perspective and the original source of mental slavery. The inability to correctly translate the outpourings of the unconscious mind into consciousness, fragmentation, gross perverted distortions and projec-tions onto the external world of one's own confused inner state of con-sciousness, is the original condition of mental slavery.

There are endless historical examples of false, self-serving, Eurocen-tric logic used to justify world-wide enslavement of African Centric people in an attempt to project the devil onto the outside world rather than deal with the devil within one's own mind. Fear and rejection of the nuances of Blackness by European-Africans caused the de-evolu-tion of many European-Africans and the original state of mental slavery. There continues to exist a great fear of African high achievement not only for fear of "genetic annhilation" but also for fear of being denied access through Daath. Present day African high achievement for many, evokes memories of past African high achievement, associated ice-age disaster memories, post-ice age jealously, and fear that their achieve ments may be stunted and undeveloped when compared with ancient African high cultures. Thus, many now ask the question, "Will all the Black men in the room please stand up?" For if we are all Africans and full of internal and external biological blackness then there is no such thing as a white man. Rather we are all Black Africans with nuances of consciousness, different pathways shaped by different geological environments that have to pass through the same Black Dot doorway to our higher selves in the same spiritual heaven.

There is great difficulty in returning to one source, Black Dot. Rodney Collin (1984) has said:

Man usually pictures his journey to the end of time as the Middle Ages pictured a journey to the end of the world. It was believed, the earth being flat, that at a certain point one must come to the edge and fall off into the unknown (Blackness). Only when a brave man held a single course and, after great hardships and strange adventures, sailed back to the same scenes from which he had set out, did they learn that the Earth was round and his course a circle.   Now we learn that time too is round, and that our voyage through it must bring us inexorably to the same years left behind. This is difficult and dangerous knowledge.   When men learned the earth was round, their sense of the known widen, but their sense of the unknown weakened.   This is the temptation of new knowledge.   The known, however strange, can never be more than zero (Black Dot) to the infinite unknown (Black Dot).   Only with this saving sense can men use strong ideas.

Certainly this is the statement from a European-African and possibly many African-Africans who have lost the ancient knowledge and thus are prisoners of illusions of time and material sense organs.   The statement does, however, point to the need to break through such limitations and return to the Black Dot source, passing through Blackness into the Primeval Waters of Nun.   For such is the passage across the abyss of Daath, the Doorway to ones own god, and higher self.

In the left upper picture of the unwrapping of the head of Pharoah Tut-ankh-Amun there appears two rope-like lawaya that separates the upper crown of the head from the lower part of the head.   Perhaps this is a symbolic reference to the lower-mind, animal and the higher-mind spiritual, dimensions of man. If this is the case, then the dark space in between the two levels would symbolically represent Blackness, as the abyss or desert that must be traversed as one moves from a lower animal, instinctual level to a higher spiritual plane. To cross such dimensions one would have to develop a greater sense of self that acknowledges the ancestors and the reality that despite great losses of material wealth of the past, something far greater than material matter survived each such event and continued on to create new material visions.

It is Blackness that heralds the birth of a new day, a new being. It is this darkness that bridges the realm of the lower animal mind, limited physical sensory organs to the higher mind, expanded consciousness and highly operative sensory perceptions. This Black inner world goes by many names (Aquarian Spiritual Center 1967), Daath, Daas, Antahkarana, Link, Bridge Between Two Worlds, The Cross, and 777. It is the attraction of Piscean age thinking, as symbolised by the Cross, that has some Africans, standing on the cross, crucified, and transfixed by it. They remain stuck in this dimension of Blackness, lost in the desert. Yet, if one is to pass through this vast Black Womb for initiation then one must develop new perceptual powers that consummates night vision and even greater vision in the day.

PART TWO

Chapter Four

URAEUS: *From Mental Slavery to Mastership I*

U raeus is a symbol for the soul, the power of the soul, or in essence, soul power. It was at least 200,000 years ago when the early Africans, the seed people of all humanity, first used the Uraeus symbol to denote man's soul. With the early African priests-scientists, the soul was not just a mere object of religious or philosophical speculation. It was, rather, the object of intense, highly disciplined, scientific study upon all conceivable subjects and possibilities of existence. Through countless years of such study, in subjects ranging from physiology to religion, the early Africans concluded that the operative quality of the soul and the essence of life energy were synonymous. The early African priests-scientists recognized commonality in the manifestation of life and soul energy upon all levels of existence (in the planets of the solar system, the sun, moon, earth, stars, galaxies and beyond; in the earth's atmosphere, seasons, animals, vegetation, minerals, land and oceans; in the core of the atom; and in those realms incomprehensible, if not imperceptible, to the physical sense organs).

Long ago, ancient Africans discovered that life energy on all planes moved along a helical-serpentine path and subsequently symbolized this notion in the form of a serpent, Uraeus. The serpent was also utilized as a symbol of the soul because it best alluded to many attributes and hidden components of the soul as well as the processes involved in its development. It was no surprise that when Western science discovered the key of life to be a chemical compound, D.N.A., the compound was found to exist in the shape of a helix, the same spiral shape formed by a snake when it sits in a coiled position.

Of particular importance to these same African scientists was the study of life energy within man, the study of the soul. They found that the image of a serpent best captured multiple operations of soul energy. This soul energy was found to travel along a path that also looked like a snake (the spine). If the energy were allowed to remain at the beginning of the path, at the base of the spinal column, then the organs located at that particular site were energized. The organs at the base of the spine are the sex organs, and when energized, produce a type of consciousness that is largely focused upon the physical plane, leaving the individual obsessed with physical desire such as indiscriminate lust, overwhelming greed, and insatiable quests for power. However, when this same energy is developed and moves upwards to the top of the spinal column. The organ at the top of the brain, the pineal gland, becomes energized, and a process that produces a higher level of consciousness in which the third eye or mind's eye becomes operative.

For the purpose of this discussion we shall use the name soul eye when referring to the third or mind's eye. Ancient African scientists found that as a person develops a soul-eye consciousness, the powers of perception become vastly magnified. This enabled the individual to perceive true reality with greater clarity. On this level, heaven was in fact tangible and frequent spiritual "highs" were not uncommon. With an operative soul-eye, the individual was reported to have developed god-like powers of intra or extra sensory perception, through the amplification of each of the five physical senses. Moreover, by having complete control of the physical body, the individual with an operative soul-eye was reported to be capable of materialization and dematerialization (teleportation).

It is with these thoughts in mind that the ancient Africans, particularly the Ethiopians and Egyptians, placed the serpent upon the crowns of their royalty. Usually the Uraeus serpent was placed over the mid-forehead, site of the pineal gland, symbolic of soul energy raised to this level and of cosmic consciousness. It was with these same thoughts in mind that the ancient Africans designed the internal structure of the Great Pyramid at Gizeh; each passageway and room is representative of a definite stage in the development of soul power. In fact, the entrance to the pyramid was aligned with the north pole star, Alpha-Draconis; a star which is part of the serpent shaped constellation, Hydra (snake). Moreover, it is the same serpent constellation, the Hydra or Pleiades, around which our sun revolves once every 25,000 years. Thus, when one considers factors such as gravitational and magnetic fields, variations in sunlight, changes in the axis of the earth's rotation, the occurrence of glacial periods, and the almost dramatic ramifications of the relationship between the sun and Pleiades system upon the earth, one can begin to grasp the significance of the innumerable factors analyzed by the African scientists.

The scope of the ancient African scientist's analyses of the soul was infinite. However, it must be realized that the greatness of their work is the by-product of highly developed soul-eyes. With their expanded levels of consciousness and faculties of perception, they produced extraordinary works, most of which are completely beyond the comprehension of today's western scientist. The average western scientist, attempting to replicate works of the ancient Africans is faced with a monumental road block, in that such an undertaking requires, as a prerequisite, a certain level of self and soul development. A scientist attempting to understand the soul must initially understand its operation within himself/herself. Such a person must fully grasp the ramifications of the serpent Uraeus, thereby experiencing certain manifestations of royalty, magicianship, priesthood and go through comprehensive phases of initiation: death, resurrection and transformation. However, only when the soul-eye level has been attained can one truly experience and make operative the foregoing: royalty being synonymous with one's ability to exercise complete control over the physical body, magicianship the ability to utilize advanced knowledge in the manipulation of energies beyond physical comprehension; and priesthood the ability to communicate with other advanced masters of vast powers, all of whom are working towards the fulfillment of soul tasks and positive growth of the universe. The African priest-scientists found that travel along the Uraeus, serpentine path would result in death or change in one's current level of consciousness. On the path, one must first be resurrected from the lower level of physical desires and become initiated through a demanding, disciplined, educational, soul-developing process which, when completed, ultimately transforms the aspirant into a master, one in full communication with his or her soul in which all things are possible.

Black people today have not yet defined their soul essence. Very few know their history, culture, language or basic physiology. Without such knowledge, the basic master plan or foundation for the scheme of things will remain a mystery. A type of slavery persists wherein the soul remains virtually imprisoned. Asa Hilliard, in his introduction to the 1970 reprint of the book, *Stolen Legacy* by George G. M. James, further defined this type of slavery as soul or self containment.

> Mental bondage is invisible violence. Formal physical slavery has ended in the United States. Mental slavery continues to the present day. This slavery affects the minds of all people, and, in one way, it is worse than physical slavery alone. That is, the person who is in mental bondage will be "self-contained." Not only will that person fail to challenge beliefs and patterns of thought which control him, he will defend and protect those beliefs and patterns of thought virtually with his last dying effort.

During the 1960's people of African descent vigorously tried to free themselves from various socio-economic conditions, only to witness a steady erosion of their hard fought gains in the 1970's. Why did this major effort go underground? Why did leaders and organizations internally "ego trip" and fight among themselves toward the ultimate formation of fragmentary organizations? Why did so much disunity prevail when the cry was for cohesiveness? Certainly, the desire to be free did exist, and the vast struggle that was launched did touch most levels of society. Why, then, did it fail? Hilliard attributes this failure to the existence of a condition of mental bondage. His basic premise is that it is the invisible violence of mental bondage that prevents our people from successfully waging a struggle to become free.

In order to see the total perspective of this premise, it is critical that we examine the term "self-containment." Websters Dictionary (1968) defines self as the identity, character or essential qualities of a person. Taking this one step further we find that identity and character is the blueprint from which one's sense of being/selfhood is developed. Containment is the policy of attempting to prevent the influence of an opposing idea, notion or political system from spreading. Thus, if all parts of a person are constructed from a basic blueprint located within the soul, then self-containment literally means prevention of the soul's blueprint from growing. Moreover, since the mind is also a part of that which is constructed, soul containment likewise stifles the growth of the mind. It is here that we can see the manner in which soul containment produces mental bondage. With soul containment, the mind is unable to develop its full capacity. The person in such condition is alienated from their soul in which lies the key for total mental as well as spiritual and physical development.

The mind can become fully developed only when life energy of the soul reaches and energizes the pineal gland. Until this occurs one cannot proceed along the serpentine path leading from physical to cosmic consciousness. While satisfying lust, greed, and power, needless in-fighting will prevent those affected from knowing their own souls and fundamental reason for existence, they cannot see their own cosmic plan nor see or respect that of others.

"One in mental slavery looks to another for guidance, instead of within. Knowledge contained in the mental slave's mind atrophies because it remains untapped."

The mental slave is self contained because he is unable to utilize the most valuable source of knowledge there is, the mind. The master, on the contrary, can use knowledge contained within his mind; the pineal gland having been energized can solve complex problems from an automatic, intuitive process; the sensory receptors are magnified to make vibratory universal rhythms tangible. Without an energized pineal gland the soul-eye remains closed. Mentally blind people of African descent are more susceptible to confusion when experiencing numerous symbols that bombard them daily. They cannot use their soul blueprints to test the validity or recognize the existence of certain fundamental symbols. They are unable to recognize the usefulness of various symbols or signatures in terms of their essential needs. In other words, Blacks, particularly in the United States, are most often unable to process cognitively that which they see, hear or otherwise feel in the everyday world. Thus, we have another critical implication about the process of moving from the condition of soul-blind to soul-eye. How does one defend against invisible violence and consequential mental

slavery? According to Yosef ben-Jochannan, another great African historian, it is through the aquisition of Knowledge, i.e., Gnosis-to know.
    Mental bondage, divorces the individual from the knowledge inherent in his being that should be used to further his evolution. One in mental slavery looks to another for guidance instead of within. The knowledge contained within the mental slave's mind has atrophied because it is untapped. When Jochannan says that it is knowledge that frees the mental slave, the implications are that one should value and adhere to one's own thoughts and feelings inherent in knowledge; one should extrapolate knowledge from every external and internal experience to excerise and cultivate the mind; thereby developing the soul.
    Again, we witness the profound wisdom of ancient African science when we recall the inscription over the entrance to the universities: "Man, Know Thy Self." Being in contact with oneself was central to all growth and development. Intimacy with the self or soul was considered fundamental for the centering and stabilizing process which anchored a central axis from which the soul could express. The theory of soul containment and the absence of self intimacy are substantiated in the freedom struggles of the 60's and 70's. There we were and here we are, struggling to be free yet unable to recognize, collectively, what we wish to liberate. It is time that we ask ourselves, "What is the self, soul or essence of Black people? What is the basis of the culture or lifestyle that Black people are attempting to perpetuate?" Truly, we cannot determine any of this until we first know ourselves as individuals and then collectively as people.
    Here we are in the 1990's desiring to be free, struggling to be liberated. We know now that knowledge is necessary but may still be uncertain as to what it is we need to learn. We need to learn first about how knowledge is being used to keep us in a hallucenagenic state of mental slavery. Knowledge that was stolen and distorted from the archives of the ancient African mystery temples. This is why the book, *Stolen Legacy* is so important and should be read from cover to cover, over and over again. It clearly shows that the foundation of all knowledge, especially that known as Greek philosophy claimed by Plato, Socrates and Aristotle, is really stolen African knowledge. Furthermore, the book outlines the ancient African educational process utilized to develop the soul. As a person moves from the condition of

mental slavery or soul-blindness, he or she must begin with the individual self and then that of the collective. By answering the question "Who am I", one formulates a concept of the self which can be used as a yardstick to measure all ideas. Consider the transformation of Malcom X from a street hustler to national leader. He developed a process where he studied ideas for their relevance to his soul. He no longer took ideas to mean what others said they meant; thus he began to extricate himself from his social conditioning. True freedom has not been achieved today because most African peoples and their leaders are virtually excommunicated from the origin of their souls. They are not in continual contact with their inner self nor with nature. Rather, they only occasionally obtain a glimpse of themselves, however, these soul visions are usually mistaken, viewed as unreal dreams or fantasies, and being viewed as such they don't come into physical manifestation. The dream is real, the failure to make the dream manifest is the fantasy.

Chapter Five

URAEUS: *From Mental Slavery to Mastership II*

S ymbols are sensory experiences which may be expressed singulary or in conjunction with any of the other physical senses. Thus, a symbol can be experienced as simply one single visual image of a picture that can be smelled, tasted, touched, or heard. While the primary tendency of most individuals is to recognize the visual aspect of a symbol, the symbol or idea has other sensory aspects. It is a compound deep structure, fabric or flesh of the mind. Symbols are memories, actual experiences witnessed by the individual. It is the meaning, understanding, perception/cognition, feeling-intuition, product, activity, or that portion of the universe which is illumined by the soul-eye, or life force. A symbol is a memory of a sensory experience organized into a gestalt or whole idea, which in itself is a building block making up the structure called the mind.

Although there are many definitions for the word symbol, the foregoing is the central concept (ideas or memories relative to a sensory experience) when energized by the fingers (external and/or internal events). For example, when one sees a snake, one automatically thinks the word "snake," the outer form having energized the mind symbol for snake and triggered a multitude of feeling tinged memories about snakes. The external snake did not have the word snake printed on it; nor did it contain feeling tinged memories of past experiences with snakes.

Ernest Jones (1948) defined the qualities of symbols as those which: (a) represent some "other" idea; (b) represent the primary element or object through some basic similarity; (c) have sensory qualities similar/ pertinent to a primary element which is abstract and/or complex; (d) make use of thought forms which are ancient, both ontogenetically and phylogenetically; (e) are a manifest expression of a hidden idea, and (f) are chosen spontaneously and unconsciously because they feel "right". Symbols have also been defined (Massey, 1974) as conscious perception of sensory experiences which is substituted for unconscious mental content. They are also seen as the basic element where indirect representations of unconscious material are: built-dreams, fantasies, hallucinations and language. Implicit in the foregoing is the idea that one root idea may be expressed as many different symbols. That is, many diversified symbols can be used to represent the same thing. This fact is due to the inherited manner in which the mind perceives or attaches meaning (i.e. ascribes symbols) to experience. Newer symbols are still related to older symbols from which they evolved just as these older symbols are related to even older symbols. For example, throughout history many different things have been used to denote food although the root meaning, nourishment, has remained unchanged, regardless of the particular culture or time period under consideration. Today, not only are there many forms of food but many symbols for it as well.

Symbols have been divided into two major types, exoteric and esoteric (Jackson, 1972; Jones, 1948; Khei, 1921; Massey, 1974). Exoteric symbols are exact, more precise and consciously representative of something. Examples can be seen in signs, figures and abbreviations used to express terms and concepts in mathematics, chemistry, physics, weights and measures, astronomy, medicine and so forth. Esoteric symbols are more implicit than exoteric symbols and are produced by deep unconscious processes. Esoteric symbols of occult, spiritual and philosophical truths have been further divided into the four following classes: geometrical, natural totemic, phallic and astrological (Khei, 1921). Geometrical esoteric symbols are believed to be those forms first utilized by man in his attempt to express ideas and communicate with others, (i.e., lines, circles, squares, triangles) (Budge, 1934). Natural-totemic, esoteric symbols are natural forms found in earthbound nature that were used to express ideas. Phallic esoteric symbols are those utilized by the ancients to denote the humans sexual organs. Astrological esoteric symbols are those utilized to express ideas and concepts relative to objects external to the planet earth. Khei (1921) has asserted that symbols were expressed in esoteric forms as a means of maintaining secrecy and social growth. It was thought necessary to conceal higher truth because the misapplication of such could liberate very potent negative energy. This was an inevitable occurrence in the hands of those lacking sufficient wisdom and will power to positively direct this liberated energy. While exoteric truth was plainly visible and accessible to the masses, esoteric truth was concealed or camoflaged through symbols decipherable only by the ancient priests-scientists.

At this point one must ask: "To what category does the symbol Uraeus, the idea of the snake belong?' In response to this most critical question we can turn to the profound statement by Gerald Massey, who maintained that the word snake is an archetypal polyglot. The snake is an ancient symbol out of which many symbols emerged and to which many are still directly related.

Words in western languages have one or two direct meanings and a greater number of figurative meanings. However, in ancient African languages works were all figurative and thus had a vast number of direct meanings. Snake was one of the earliest words. At a point in time, almost every object on earth or the heavens was labeled, "serpent." Some of the objects named serpent were: woman, hawk, egg, wolf, milk, bear, crocodile, scorpion, seven headed cobra, apple tree, pyramid, earth, atmospheric conditions, darkness, rainbow, thunder, lightning, moon, pole stars draconis, wisdom, soul, evil, good, magic, hole, peacock's tail, self, exlixer, shadow, resurrection, life, kundalini, third eye, time, and the elementary gods of Egypt, earth (Bata), fire (heh and Kheh), and air (Nef) and water (Hydra) (Massey, 1974). As the archetypal polyglot, the universal symbol Uraeus represents the operation of the supreme duality between: God and gods (angels), the macrosom-microcosm, esoteric-exoteric, invisible-visible, ideal-material, spirit-matter, inner-outer, chaos-order, truth-illusion, all-part, unknown-known, good-bad, pure-impure, total consciousness-limited consciousness, knowledge-ignorance and master-slave.

God is defined in Black Gnostic Studies (1967) as a hierarchy of energies-electrical, magnetical, gravitational and nuclear, as well as spiritual (mental). Types of energy differ only in their rate of vibration or speed of movement. The faster the speed of energy, the wider its sphere of influence and the greater the number of planes or levels of consciousness upon which it operates. The slowest moving energy is crystallized as matter, the fastest moving energy is spirit or mind. Mental slaves are ignorant and blind because their sense receptors are undeveloped, and unable to accurately call forth symbols activated by internal and external events. Such individuals have not turned on spiritual energies. They hear only static (confusion) and are unable to read the symbols contained within their mind. Masters, on the other hand, through the education-esoteric process, have sharpened all of their sense receptors, and consequently are able to focus upon the whole of their being, right, left brain-mind; wherein is contained the basic blueprint for existence. Focus upon one's all, enables one to see the total spectrum with the soul-eye; all vibratory speeds and all spiritual energies. Energy can produce change by transforming symbols or ideas.

This idea that the name Uraeus is a symbol of God, and all spiritual energies, can be seen with closer analysis of the name URAEUS. The divinity was symbolized by the serpent, which was called by several names. One such name was "Arat," which meant cobra to the ancient Egyptians. The Egyptian hieroglyphic depiction of the name for Uraeus is given below (Massey, 1976):

Fig. 2   Uraeus = 〰〰 = Arat

Fig. 3   = Ra

Another, far more widely used name was "Uraeus," the subject of this discussion. Its relationship to the Egyptian God Ra can be seen in the Hieroglyphics for the latter. It was the Uraeus or snake deity which was worshipped in ancient Egypt as a sign of sovereignty and royalty (Black Gnostic Studies 1967).

E.A. Budge has written a detailed historical review of the early African use of the Uraeus symbol. This critically important review is readily available in a paperback version of his book, *The Gods of Egyptians,* Volumes I and II. Contained within this account is a description of Uraeus' ancient usage: in the representation of god's duality (vulture/serpent); during coronation ceremonies of the Egyptian priests-kings (pharoahs); in the embalming of the dead or preparation of mummies and its relationship to the eye of Horus, heaven and the human head. It is upon this excellent historical account of Uraeus that we will now base this section of Uraeus, Part II.

In ancient times Uraeus was known as the goddess Uatchet, who was closely associated with the goddess Nekhebet. Both were sometimes depicted as a serpent or Uraeus. So ancient was their use that Budge (1969) asserts that they were used in the archaic period. By archaic it is meant that they were used in Egypt at a predynastic time before the first recorded pharoah, before 3,200 B.C. Budge states:

From the hieroglyphic inscriptions which belong to the archaic period we find that the Kings of Egypt were in the habit of placing before their names the sign (Uraeus symbol), by which they intended to indicate their sovereignty over the south and North.

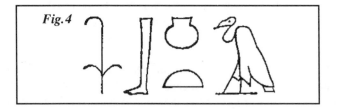

Fig. 4

The vulture goddess was often referred to as the Goddess of the South, Nekhebet. She was worshipped throughout upper Egypt in the city called Nekhebet by the Egyptians, which was, moreover, the capital of the third nome. This same city was called Eileithyiaspolis and "Civitas Lucinae" by the Greeks and Romans, respectively. The shrine of the Goddess Nekhebet, Nekhent, is presently located in the current Arab village of el-Kab. Nekhebet was also believed to be the daughter of Ra, the divine wife of Khent Amenti, the holy vulture, and Hathor. The serpent goddess, Uatchet was worshipped throughout Lower or Northern Egypt, particularly in the city of Per-uatchet, the capital of the seventh nome (city). This city of Uraeus worship, as well as the other sites of its worship, were collectively known as Pe-tep; within which were two distinct divisions. The first group, Tep was identified with Isis and

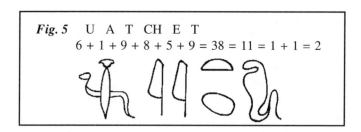

Fig. 5   U   A   T   CH   E   T
6 + 1 + 9 + 8 + 5 + 9 = 38 = 11 = 1 + 1 = 2

Uatchet-Horus was the primary deity. Uatchet was regarded as the goddess of the elements and months of the Egyptians year (Epiphu), and during later dynastic times, was given the name Ap-tavi (Budge, 1968). It can be seen that Nekhebet is directly related to the earlier Uatchet symbol by virtue of its derivation/evolution.

From the Black Gnostic Studies, Esoteric Tarot Chart (1967) we can find the numerical value for UATCHET (Fig.5). Correspondence for the number 2 are the degree path 1, sacred tarot-The Magician, signature of letter-House, Hebrew-Beth, Hebrew sign, English value -B, royal crown. Moreover, upon the forehead of the royal crown were most often found two serpents; one being Uatchet or Uraeus and the other, Nekhebet, symbolized not as a vulture but instead in the Uraeus, serpentine form.

Budge, has offered several interpretations for some of the multiple meanings of Nekhebet and Uatchet. Basically both of the goddesses were depicted as serpents. Over the right or south side of the door the serpent Nekhebet was placed. Over the left or north side was the serpent Uatchet. This placement symbolized the astronomical correlation drawn between Nekhebet and the Western or right eye of the Sun (daughter/son) during the latter's journey through the underworld and that drawn between Uatchet and the Eastern or left eye. As an earth bound nature symbol, the Uatchet-Nekhebet powers/goddesses/serpents were seen as fertile nature goddesses, father of fathers, mother of mothers, who existed from the beginning, the creator of the world. The Uatchet-Nekhebet powers were also viewed as the mother of the Sun-God, Ra, and because of this as the mother or the nurse and protectorof the kings of Egypt who were believed to be the sons of the Sun-God Ra. Thus, the Uraeus symbol is often synonymous to Horus.

The Uatchet-Nekhebet Uraeus symbol was a central feature in coronation ceremonies of Egyptian kings or pharoahs. Coronations were not mere political events but rather religious-scientific affairs; These events celebrated the King's position as a priest instructed in greater knowledge of the priesthood, further evidenced by name changing ceremonies (Budge, 1967). For example, King "Tut" was named Tut-ankh-Aton before his coronation and Tut-ankh-Amen afterwards. The name change emphasized his priestly elevation. It is very probable that part of the coronation process took place within temples that contained sanctuaries of the gods Uatchet and Nekhebet. Uatchet resided in a chamber on the west or right side of the sanctuary called "pernesert" or house of fire. Nekhebet, resided in the chamber on the east or left side of the sanctuary which was called "per ur" or great house. Budge asserts,

> It is very probable that at the time of coronation of a King, priestesses dressed themselves in the character of the two goddesses; one declared the south had been given to him whilst the other asserted the same concerning the North.

Uatchet-Nekhebet's powers were also centrally involved in the process of embalming the dead or mummification. Concerning this, Budge refers to M. Maspero's *Memories sur quelques Papyrus,* wherein it is stated that,

> ...the goddess Uatchet cometh unto thee in the form of the Underworld, and would change their faces into things of beauty with two brilliant eyes of light. To make certain this result, the 'bandage of Nekheb' was laid upon the forehead of every carefully prepared mummy.....goddess Uatchet cometh unto thee in the form of living Uraeus to anoint thy head with their flames. She riseth up on the leftside of thy head, and she shineth from the right side of thy temples without speech; they rise upon thy head during each and every hour of theday, even as they do for their father Ra, and through them the terror which thou inspirest in the holy spirits is increased, and because Uatchet and Nekhebet rise up on thy head, and because thy brow becometh the portion of thy head whereon they establish themselves, even as they do upon the brow of Ra, and because they never leave thee, awe of thee striketh into the souls which are

made perfect. I am Horus, and I have come forth from the Eye of Horus (i.e. Ra), I am Uatchet who come forth from Horus. I am Horus, and I fly up and perch myself upon the forehead of Ra in the bows of his boat which is in heaven" The deceased is said to be the lord of Maat, which the goddess Uatchet worketh. "I am the spiritual body of the lord of Maat which is made by the goddess Uatchet.

Continued examination of the name URAEUS reveals that it is composed of the syllables or sounds U-RAE-US. The "Rae" relates to Ra or the Egyptian god Ra, the all, the Big God. "Us" relates to human individuals, literally. Thus, U-RAE-US represents the god within us. In other words, URAEUS represents an individual's ability to utilize innate god-like power or knowledge of all symbols through the development of all of sensory receptors in such a manner that he or she is able to tune into all energies, especially the rapid spiritual energies upon which the all total God communicates.

Robert Hoffstein (1975) has defined several of the Eastern ideas behind the letter U. The negative energy of "U" refers to ideas that are negative as seen in the prefix "Un." It represents the idea without meaning, knowledge, unknown ignorance. On the other hand, the positive energy of the letter "U" refers to that which binds something to another, as in the word unity. Overall, we can now discern the esoteric or inner meaning of the idea URAEUS. "U" is either that which binds or that which is unknown or does not bind. "RA" represents God, while "US" literally refers to us, the cultural collective of individuals humans. Knowledge is the process. Lack of soul knowledge, on the other hand, prevents the realization of the God-like powers within the individual.

Gerald Massey (1974), author of the outstanding classical review, *Typology of the Mythical Serpent,* said in reference to the origin of the name serpent, that the name is pre-eminently inner African. Below are two listings of the names of serpents based upon his classification.

Non-African
Snake-English   Nachash-Hebrew
Naga-Sanskrit   Naya-Arabic
Neke and Nakahi-Maori

African

Nyoka-Kanyika	Nyoka-Nyombe	Nyoka-Kisam
Nyoka-Kabenda	Nyoka-Basunde	Nyoka-Nyamban
Nyoka-Mimboma	Nyoka-N'gola	Noga-Basuto
Nyoka-Musentandu	Nyoka-Zubalo	Nyoke-Swahili
Nyoka--Kasands	Nyoka-Songa	

Massey maintained that the Y in the names is not a primary sound, but rather one that evolved from g. The Nk or Ng is the original African sound. In the Nk or Ng form, the name for serpent exists in hieroglyphics where Nkaka is synonymously interchanged with Naka and in the Egyptian hymn to Amen-Ra, the Sun God is said to send his arrows against the evil serpent Naka.

To illustrate the universality of the serpent symbol Uraeus, we will now review several uses of the symbol in an esoteric, geometrical, natural totemic, phallic, astrological form.

As a geometical symbol, the serpent was pictured as swallowing its tail to form a circle. The Egyptians use the circle to represent the serpent because they believe that the serpent's body had no appendage other than the head with it's mouth. Thus all circular objects were named serpents. It is also interesting to note that a serpent sitting in a coiled or spiral position can be viewed as several circles juxaposed one on top of the other.

Looking at natural totemic symbols the snake found in nature, we have several important considerations. Lightning was considered a serpent because of its zig-zag movement across the sky which was similar to the zig-zag movement of a snake across the ground. Lightning also makes a hissing type of sound like the sound made by snakes. The rainbow was considered serpent of the sky. Women were serpents because they experienced a 28 day mentrual cycle like the 28 day cycle of the moon, another circular shaped object already named serpent. The head of the serpent represented the first 14 days of the waning or descending phase. Time was named serpent because it measured change from night to day based upon the interplay of two circular, serpentine objects, the sun and moon. Even milk, a product of mammalian animals, was named serpent as it was produced by women who had been transformed into mother's following nine months (nine lunar or serpentine cycles) of gestation of the fetus (Massey, 1974).

Most importantly the serpent displayed attributes that were similar to the operation of the mind. Snakes were seen to be able to shed their skins and transform into a new skin, leaving behind the old, dead skin. This process was likened to the tranformation which takes place when the individual transforms and leaves behind the dead state of consciousness of mental slavery and moves into a new state of soul eye or mastership. Snakes were able to stare at their prey and mesmerize it in a trance so they could move in and swallow it. Mesmerization has often been deemed the use of mind control; the use of invisible, rapidly moving energy too fast for the physical eye to see. It also alludes to the master individual's capacity to hold a symbol still and thereby focus on it in order to swallow or understand the whole of its meaning.

Phallic associations with serpents are all too obvious. The male sex organ, the penis, is shaped like a snake and just as some snakes spurt out a white milky fluid that affects life (poison-death), so does the male penis spit out a white milky fluid that affects life (sperm-life). Women also possess a snake-like sex organ, the clitorus. The female vaginal tract into which the male penis enters is a long tract like a snake as is the long tube shaped uterus, the organ at the end of the vaginal tract, which is the actual womb of life. Thus the reproductive organs of both males and females are all serpentine in structure; those of the male projecting outward, and the major portion of the female's projecting inward.

The astronomical, esoteric-symbolic use of the snake was defined in an earlier section where it was stated that the sun and moon, being circular, represented the circular mouth of the serpent and were named serpent. The different seasons of the year could be predicted by observing the movement of the sun. Furthermore, longer periods of time in which there were major cyclical changes in rain fall patterns and glacial periods due to shifts in the earth's polar axis were measured by the sun. It took almost 26,000 years to circle the relative central star system, the Pleaides. Again, the months were measured by lunar cycles, seasons by sun cycles and geological and glacial periods by star cycles.

Finally, another way of analyzing the word Uraeus is to look at its numerical value; the idea being that similar ideas have similar vibratory rates or numerical correspondences. This is an important way for us to further explore the manner in which many ideas are related to the Uraeus concept. The first letter of Uraeus is U, the 21st letter of the

English alphabet. Twenty-one is produced by multiplying 3 times 7. Twenty-one can also be expressed as 2 = 1 or 3, which again is the triad concept of Uraeus (e.g., total God = Good God = Bad God).

From the Black Gnostic Study (1967) material we can explore a number of ideas which pertain to the number 21. The "Macrocosmic Man Chart" relates the number 21 to the third decanate of Scorpio, the musical note C, the 2nd lumbar of the spinal vertebra, the 21st masonic degree and masonic name ??? Prussian Knight. "The Microcosmic Man Chart" draws an analogy between the number twenty-one and the astrological sign Scorpio, instinct-pugnacity, urge-aggressive, positive instinct-occult understanding, and negative instinct-death, misused sex.

Aleister Crowley's (1970) book, 777, provides a list of numerical correspondences which links many different symbols to their equivalent root meanings based upon their numerical values. Considering the root idea of Uraeus to be a serpent, Crowley's book defines its numerical equivalent as nineteen (19). Nineteen corresponds to the astrological sign Leo (ruled by the sun, center, King) general attribute of Egyptian Gods (Horus), Queen Scale of Colour (deep purple or black), Greek God Demeter (borne by lions), precious stones (cat's eyes), plants (sunflower), Roman God or Venus (repressing the Fire of Vulcan), magical powers (western mysticism), training wild beasts and magical weapons (The Discipline). We have shown that the worship of the serpent in Egypt is ancient. Even before the time of the recorded dynasties in Egypt, the serpent was well established and worshipped as a symbol of God. In predynastic times ancient Egypt was divided into two Kingdoms, a northern and southern kingdom or lower and upper Egypt. Upper Egypt worshipped primarily the vulture which later became the hawk. Lower Egypt worshipped the serpent or Uraeus. The great center of Uraeus worship existed in the Nile Delta of Lower Egypt at the city named "Per-Uatchet or Uatchet." The vulture, on the other hand, was worshipped at the city called Nekhebet. The Uraeus god was called "Uatchet" and the vulture god "Nekhebet" or Nekhebit." During the early dynastic period the kings proclaimed their sovereignty over both Upper Egypt and Lower Egypt by naming themselves the "Lord of the Shrine of the Vulture and Uraeus" (Budge, 1969). Thus in ancient Egypt, the Uraeus was a symbol of divinity and royalty. Ancient Egyptians pictured their god Ra wearing two Uraeus serpents on his forehead. Whereas, the enemy of the god Ra was the evil serpent Apap or Typhon (Massey, 1974). The early Africans depicted two serpents, the good serpent Uraeus and the bad serpent Apap. It is a statement of mental slavery that today's Black African knows only of the bad serpent and is without knowledge of the true god as symbolized by Uraeus, the good.

By studying ideas for their relevance to individual life, one no longer takes things to mean what others say they mean. The self can be extricated from the web of slavery type social conditioning. True freedom has not been achieved today because many African peoples and their leaders are excommunicated from their souls. They are not in continual contact with their inner selves nor with nature. Rather, they only occasionally seek a glimpse of themselves. Their soul vision contains a film over it and the reality is seen as unreal. As such reality is not brought into physical manifestation. The dream is real, the failure to make it manifest is the unreality. There we were and here we are, struggling to be free yet unable to define the essence of that which we wish to liberate. It is time that we ask ourselves, "What is the self, soul, or essence of Black People?" What is the basis of the cultural life style that Black people are attempting to perpetuate? Truly, we cannot determine any of this until we first know ourselves as individuals and then collectively as a people.

Chapter Six

URAEUS: *From Mental Slavery to Mastership III*

T he Uraeus-pineal gland is the third eye, good serpent and key to the unconscious mind. It is the key to a level of conscious awareness, vision and understanding that becomes increasingly operative during the ascension of an individual from lower levels of mental slavery (un-awareness or ignorance, undeveloped unconscious) to higher levels of mastership. A study of the Uraeus-pineal gland relationship clearly reveals highly advanced ancient and African scientific knowledge of pineal anatomy: It was understood that pineal anatomy was significantly influenced by sunlight, darkness, the unconscious, ascension and black-ness, melanin or skin color.

In the removal of the chains of mental slavery it is essential that one knows the history of African scientific achievements. Science is knowledge. A slave has little knowledge and consequently is less in control of his or her own life, dominated by others and the immediate environment. Today's mental slave of African descent is afraid of science, fearful that he or she lacks the mind power to gain and utilize such knowledge. Today's mental slave of African descent still believes in the European, who promotes such lies as: European science is the most advanced the world has ever seen; the European logical style is best for scientific study while the intuitive style, and spiritual mind of the African is inferior or incapable of the same. Today's mental slave of African descent is ignorant of the vastness of the Stolen Legacy, unaware that the source of 'so-called' western science is African.

Perhaps, some of the fear Africans have in studying science is that science in European schools is usually super-concentrated on the logical approach. The African student senses the emphasis on logic at the neglect of sentiment; a fact that is most troublesome in that the feeling-intuitive approach is the core of African essence (King, Lewis, Dixon, Nobles, 1976). African science emphasizes a holistic approach, a combination of feelings and logic, material and ideal, and the scientific and religious. It, in fact, actually gives material and proof of religious/spiritual concepts. The African scientist first feels intuitively and then tempers it with what he/she knows logically, whereas the European first thinks logically and then ignores his/her feelings. To break the barrier of mental slavery today those of African descent must learn the truth of great ancient African scientific achievements and thereby come to realize that, without question, they have the brain power to continue in the same vein.

Importantly, the Uraeus-pineal relationship reveals ancient African science to be as advanced if not beyond today's western science in the areas of anatomy, chemistry, physiology, psychology, sociology, education, astrophysics, astronomy, physics and biology. As mentioned Ancient African science differs from today's Western science, in that the former placed a strong emphasis on the ideas of religion, spirituality and psychology. For the African, science and religion were one just as mind and body were one. African science used not only logical yardsticks to measure scientific observations but also emotional, intuitive and spiritual ones.

African science defined as "best" those relationships (mental conditions) between one's soul (self) and one's environment which transformed both. During such personal transformations the African scientists became more sensitive and better able to make hidden unconscious ideas conscious. So transformed, the African scientists experienced heaven on earth through an ascension to a higher level of consciousness wherein they experienced frequent "best" emotions (spiritual highs) and "best" ideas (illumination, raised unconscious ideas). Together, the "best" emotions and "best" ideas enabled the transformed scientists to be in continuous harmony and rhythm with their individual souls and environment.

The Ancient African scientists achieved knowledge required for harmonic union with soul (self) and environment through the opening of the pineal, which is the key to the transformative unconscious, the infinite cosmic computer. This biological computer of life was itself the essence of godhood in humans, infinite, omnipotent, omnipresent; an endless source of knowledge where all emerged, adhering to universal law and justice.

Anatomically, the pineal is part of the brain. It is a structure found in the middle of the brain that forms part of the floor of the third ventricle (Chusid, 1967; Mess, 1975; Wurtman, 1977). From a side view of the head it is found approximately midway between the forehead and back of the head. From a front view of the head the pineal appears as a structure in the middle of the forehead. It is clearly evident that Africans were fully aware of pineal anatomy for they depicted the pineal as a serpent, Uraeus, in the middle of the forehead, the anatomical site of the pineal gland. There are many African references to the Uraeus forehead site. A few examples of this description were given in Uraeus Part II. Another important reference is found in the Book of the Coming forth By Day (Budge, 1967):

> I am Horus and and I have come forth from the Eye of Horus (Uraeus-Pineal Gland). I am Uatchet who comes forth from Horus. I am Horus and I fly up and perch myself upon the forehead of Ra in the bows of his boat which is in heaven.

This reference suggests that a key to heaven could be found in the forehead, wherein lies the pineal gland or Uraeus.

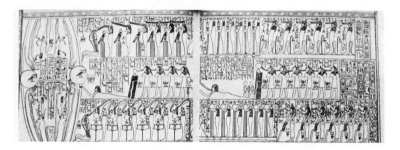

Fig. 6 The Shrine of Tut-Ankh-Amun, Piankoff, Alexander

African Knowledge of the Pineal Relationship to Sunlight and Darkness

Physiologically, the operation and function of the pineal gland is directly related to sunlight and darkness (Wurtman, 1977; King, 1977). During darkness the pineal releases the powerful hormone melatonin,

a chemical related to brain function (Carman, 1976). Melatonin is released
into the brain in eight intervals between the hours of 11 p.m. and 7 a.m.,
the hours of darkness. Again, there are numerous African references to
the pineal relationship to sunlight, darkness, and the hours of the day. If
one knows that the sun was named Ra, then one can appreciate this fact
(Budge, 1967),

> She (Uatchet, Uraeus or Pineal) riseth up on the left side of thy
> head during each and every hour of the day, even as they do for
> their father Ra (the sun).

An important reference is present in Genesis 32:31, "And as he (Jacob)
passed over Peniel the sun rose upon him, and he halted upon his thigh."
It is not surprising that the Bible is closely related to Africa and African
science. The great African historian Dr. Yosef ben-Jochannan has clearly
pointed out that Christianity and African religion are to each other as a
child is to its parents. Christianity was derived from African religion. Dr.
Ben Jochannan provides a wealth of information on this subject in, *The
Black Man's Religion and Extracts and Comments from the Holy Black
Bible and The Black Clergy Without a Black Theology.*

Another critical insight into the relationship between African religion
and Christianity is found in the book, *Stolen Legacy*, by George G. M.
James:

> Ancient Rome, through edicts of her Emperors Theodosius in
> the 4th centry A.D. and Justinian in the 6th century A.D.
> abolished the Mysteries of the African Continent; that is the
> ancient culture system of the world. The higher metaphysical
> doctrines of those Mysteries could not be comprehended; the
> spiritual powers of the priest were unsurpassed; the magic of
> the rites and ceremonies filled the people with awe; Egypt was
> the holy land of the ancient world; and the Mysteries were the
> one ancient Catholic religion whose power was supreme. This
> lofty culture system of the Black people are depised; because
> they are all offspring of the African Mysteries, which have
> never been clearly understood by Europeans and consequently
> have provoked their prejudice and condemnation.

The relationship between Uraeus and sunlight is shown in a hieroglypic table from King Tut's tomb which depicts a serpent putting sunlight (rainbow spectrum of colors) into the pineal forehead, and a star (sun) engaged in a similar operation (Fig. 7).

African Knowledge of the Pineal Relationship to Blackness/Melanin

Many Africans believe in the concept of the underworld or Amenta. Everything that was of the underworld was painted Black. The modern name for the underworld is the unconscious mind. The pineal gland, through its hormone serotonin or melatonin, is a key to the unconscious (Carman, 1976; King, 1967; Moskovits, 1978; Schneider, 1975; Filators, 1976; Forrest, 1975; King, 1977). It unlocks the unconscious mind and makes it accessible to the aspirant. Uraeus, the pineal gland, enables one to utilize the eye of Horus to envision the unconscious; thereby greatly expanding one's comprehension or level of consciousness.

Recent discoveries by Western scientists have found that the pineal hormone melatonin produces extraordinary changes in the mind. The magnitude of these changes is dependent upon the sensitivity of the individual. When melatonin was given to "normal" people, they experience an increase in tranquility, sleep or dreams. When melatonin was given to "psychologically abnormal" people they experienced a return of depression or schizophrenia. Since sleep and dreams are the royal road to the unconscious, the manner in which the pineal produces chemical keys to unlock the unconscious mind should be more apparent.

Most importantly, the Uraeus-pineal relationship to skin color is found in the pineal hormone melatonin released during darkness. Melatonin is also a hormone that controls the production of melanin

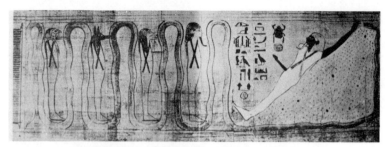

Fig. 8 Egyptian Religious Texts and Representations, vol. 3

(black color) in the skin. With this in mind we can perhaps have a greater appreciation for the African drawing of a black mummy moving into the black underworld of Amenta-black chemicals (Uraeus-pineal hormone melatonin) unlocking the doorway to the unconscious. It is also of interest that the mummy is shown with an erect black penis. One possible explanation of this factor could be the fact that the male or female sex organ, being one of the blackest parts of the body, must contain the greatest number of black pigment cells, melanocytes. During the dream phase of sleep, when penile (serpent) erection occurs in males and clitoral (serpent) erection occurs in females, it is only a natural process during the hours of darkness, during the hours when melatonin is actively being secreted into the brain or during those hours which Western science had labeled REM sleep (i.e., that portion of sleep wherein the individual, via dreams, peers into the unconscious).

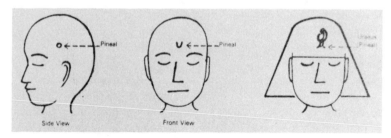

Fig. 9 Uraeus, vol. 3

African Knowledge of the Pineal Relationship to the Process of Transformation and the Ascension from Salvery to Godhood

Ancient African science further defined the Uraeus, pineal or serpent in the head (brain) as a key to one's own individual godhood and unlimited powers. In Genesis 32:27-32, It was at the place named Peniel (pineal gland) that Jacob (a mental slave, dwelling in ignorance, symbolic of the undeveloped unconscious) met the angel of God (mastership, infinite knowledge). During the wrestling bout which ensued, he ascended from his former state of lower consciousness and was transformed into Israel (higher self). It was at Peniel that Jacob saw God face to face and his life was renewed: "And Jacob called the name of the place Peniel, for I have seen God face to face, and my life is preserved," (Genesis 32:30). Heaven was believed to be in the head. Thus a higher level of consciousness was to be attained by utilizing the pineal gland to unlock the unconscious, effecting a harmonic relationship between self and environment (darkness-light).

African Knowledge of the Importance of the Mind, Unconscious, Symbols and Mythology

Africans studied the mind and named it nous (James, 1976). Africans studied the unconscious part of the mind and named it Amenta or the underworld. Africans studied symbols and named them archetypes (Jochannan, 1970; McGinness, 1973). The unconscious is the great internal reservoir of infinite knowledge (Assagioli, 1965) that each person has the potential to possess. It is the full knowledge of the operation and utilization of the universal hierarchy of energies.

Africans also studied mythology, fables on an exoteric level which contain hidden formulae on an esoteric level. Mythology provides a clue into the particular relationship a symbol or idea must establish with other related ideas before a synthesis can occur. Synthesis is the key to ascension. An example of a particular type of synthesis can be seen in the African myth of Osiris, Isis and Horus as well as in its Christian counterpart, that of Joseph, Mary and Jesus. Osiris represents the masuline left brain cortical hemisphere (logic). Isis represents the feminine, right brain cortical hemisphere (intuition). The child Horus was produced by the union or synthesis of Osiris and Isis and exemplified a balance between feeling and logic.

Human mythology began with the serpent, an archetypal polygot image of God. The human race, having originated in Africa, migrated across the entire world. Each migratory wave carried with it a common form of serpent mythology. The book, *Encircled Serpent,* by M. Oldfield Howey, contains many records of the history of serpent mythology. From this book one can review several of the serpent myths:

> Thoth, also known as Athoh, thaut or teuth, founded the first colonies in this country after the flood, and taught the Egyptian to worship Kneph, the original Spirit, pervading all creation under the symbol of a serpent.

Thoth was symbolized as a serpent, and has been named Hermes-Trismegistus by the Greeks, and Mercury by the Romans (Howey, 1955).

> We many find him as Buddha in India; as Zoroaster in Persia; Osiris in Egypt; Thoth in Phoenica (Africa); Hermes or Cadmus in Greece, and Odin in Scandinavia. Pharoah, Phra or Aphra is said to be compounded of Aphe, "serpent," and Ra, the sun, from where they decended.

> Indian mythology centers around the Krishna, an incarnation of Vishnu, Sun God, who went into the river Yamuna, home of the terrible serpent Kayla (evil spirit with a thousand heads) and engaged in great combat with the serpent. The serpent entwined about Krishna's body, but the divine child became so large that Kayla had to release him allowing Krishna to tear off the hydra's heads one by one.

> In Buddhism, two dragons are fabled to have descended from the clouds to bathe, the divine babe, Sakya Budda at his birth. One was sprouting warm water and the other cold. He was addressed by his disciples as Mahanago, or Great Naga serpent. Even in the time of the Chinese pilgrims, Buddhists Sramanas were worshipping the Naga serpent, and celebrating the ritual at Naga serpent Temples.

Among the Aztecs he was named Quetzacoatl, the Serpent, and was regarded as an incarnation of the "Serpent Son," the feathered serpent was his symbol. To this day the Hopi Indians of Mexico symbolize the Sun as a serpent with its tail in its mouth.

The Warramunga Tribe of North Central Australia has conceived a huge mythological totem serpent, the sire of all snakes. It lives in a waterhole, and if offended, it may emerge to destroy human beings, so must be treated with gret respect.

The central theme of the serpent myths in cultures throughout the world reflects their common parent and central germ, the African serpent myth of Osiris. The Sun God Ra was also named Osiris and in African mythology was said to have suffered a cruel death on earth but by his divine power rose again in a glorified body. This myth funtioned to give the Egyptians their belief in resurrection. The serpent's periodical casting off of its old skin furnished an illustration of this allegory.

Again it is important to recall that Uraeus, the serpent, the pineal gland, is also named the Eye of Horus. It is important to recall that the pineal gland is in the midline between the left cortical hemisphere and the right cortical hemisphere. The developed pineal establishes a balance between the male and female parts of one's consciousness. Africans believed that the unlimited power of individual godhood occurs with "one who sees God." In other words, new power and new life come about through the union of the masculine (Shiva or Anima) and the feminine (Shakti or Animus) principles.

African science is infinite; a product of thousands of years of study by highly advanced African scientists, each operative at the godhead level.

Chapter Seven

URAEUS: *From Mental Slavery To Mastership IV*

A ccording to the Honorable Elijah Muhammed the following message was given to him by Fard D. Muhammed: "We believe in the resurrection of the dead-not in physical resurrection but in mental resurrection. We believe that the so-called Negroes are most in need of
mental resurrection, therefore, they will be resurrected best." Most
black people are dead today, because they don't have control of their
own mind. They do not know how their mind operates and so they would
rather allow their slave master to think for them. Many black people are
so mentally dead that they are actually anti-intellectual, afraid to read,
afraid to materialize their own dreams and intuitions. They both, run
from school and allow school to miseducate them. It is a false
expectation to believe that the same slave master, who, during the time
of physical slavery made it a crime to teach Black people to read or
count, would now allow adequate schools for the development of the
Black mind. The failure of today's schools to educate the Black mind
is not the problem, rather it is the slave master's designed solution to the
problem, the process of "self containment," and the intentional perpetu-
ation of mental slavery after the removal of physical slavery.
    The Black mind has been put to sleep and kept undeveloped in
today's educational system. Vast numbers of Black students are
programmed to give up, early, on the very knowledge that the slave
master uses to rule. "I can't read, I can't count, math is too hard, that
book is too thick, I don't want to be an egg head scientist, physics is for
white people, that is the man's science, the man's science is too heavy
for us, it is too abstract, I don't have time, I'm a slow learner, I was told
that I should try something easier, I don't do well on tests, school will

take too long, I'm bored, I just want to have a good time," etc. This list is endless of the lies that we have been told or tell ourselves to continue mental slavery. Some Black students who do well in school also remain mental slaves, for they function as the modern overseer of the ghetto, (plantation), for the modern slave master. These trained students lack an understanding of how to use knowledge for themselves individually and collectively for their people. They can become as brutal as the slave master and remained tragically pained by their dilemma without the will power to transform themselves or participate in the transformation of their collective Black people. Conversely, an "awake" Black person is in control of their mind and by definition will always use their knowledge to transform self in the constant pursuit of spiritual and material unity. It is not enough just to know something. One must have enough knowledge to bring about change, real change, transformative change.

The point is, Black people must educate themselves. They cannot expect the mental slave master to educate them for several reasons. First, it is against the interest of the mental slave master to adequately educate Black people because he would deplete his ability to siphon off Black skills. Second, the mental slave master profoundly fears Black revenge, for centuries of abominable treatment. Third, the mental slave master is extremely afraid of the power of the Black mind and Black genuis that produced highly advanced cultures and scientific achievements in the past and present. Fourth, the mental slave master does not know how to educate the Black mind. The advanced psychology required for training the Black mind, despite being stolen by Europeans and Asians, was seldom understood. For many of those who stole the legacy of African achievement were afraid to elevate their own minds to the level of Uraeus, soul (mind) power that was achieved by African intellectual & spiritual advancement. According to Wallis Budge (1969), late European keeper of stolen Egyptian antiquities.

The evidence on the subject now available indicates that he (Greek or Roman) was racially incapable of appreciating the importance of such beliefs (Egyptian religion science) to those who held them, and although, as in the case of Ptolemies, he was ready to tolerate, and even, for state purposes, to adopt them, it was impossible for him to absorb them into his life.

For African people to break the chains of mental slavery they must use and update the same methods that ancient Africans effectively used in their University, Mystery System. African people need not be confused about the transformative process. No amount of mystification, random discovery, hit and miss research, will instantly define a process that developed over thousands of years. African people can update their elaborative transformative process by understanding that Uraeus is a symbol for the process. The transformation of African mental slaves into Africans with self-mastery is a worldwide process of returning to formulative history and records of past achievements, not to copy exact duplicates but to reclaim that which is of value and which can still be used, with modification in today's world. *The Black person who embraces their historical Blackness has the key to transforming the Black mind.* In, *Stolen Legacy,* Dr. James presents a critical reference,

> The Egyptian Mysteries (University) had three grades of student (1) The Mortals: probationary students who were being instructed, but who had not yet experienced inner vision; (2) The Intelligences: those who had attained the inner vision, and had received mind or Nous, and; (3) The Creators or Sons of Light: those who had become united with the Light (i.e., true spiritual consciousness). These grades are described as equivalents of Initiation, Illumination and Perfection.

James recounts how the ancient Africans considered the differences between a mental slave and a mental master. The Master possessed mind, nous and awareness of the unconscious, Amenta (Infinite personal resevoir of knowledge), whereas the mental slave did not.

The unconscious mind or Amenta is contained within the mind of every person. We are all latent with undeveloped genius, undeveloped infinite and immortal universal computers. The unconscious mind by definition means that consciousness or knowledge which we are unaware of. This concept stresses the vast importance of the inscription over the entrance to all ancient African universities, "Man Know Thy Self." In other words, the knowledge of the university was already inside of every person from birth. The purpose of the education was to draw the knowledge out rather than pour it in. Thus, African People will not be intellectually and spiritually liberated until they can look within.

The Self, Soul and Essence of Black People

It is time that we ask ourselves, "What is the self, soul or essence of Black people? What is the basis of the culture, and life style that Black people are attempting to perpetuate? Truly, we cannot determine any of this until we first know ourselves as individuals and then collectively as people. Our goal now is to provide insight into spiritual methods which one can use to draw out one's soul, tap the energy therein and know the God within us. The self, soul and essence of Black people is the Black mind. From an Ancient African psychological perspective a mental slave operates at the concrete-mind level and defines as reality only those things which can be perceived by the five physical senses-vision, hearing, smell, touch and taste. However, this is an inadequate operative mode for two reasons. First, the physical sense receptors have activation ranges, a certain range of energies or vibratory frequencies that record sensory experiences. If the energy is either faster or slower than the receptor's range, the person is unaware or unconscious of the experience. Secondly, a mental slave uses less than 10% of his/her entire brain. The other 90% remains undeveloped and unconscious. A Master, uses the undeveloped sense receptors, the physical sense receptor activation ranges are expanded and undeveloped brain cells are developed. Ancient African psychology held that there were seven levels of the mind and a central point. The central point was named the Black Dot, the spirit or atomic egg from which the soul, mind and body evolved. Albert Churchward (1976) defines the Black Dot as "Here, then, we have the original dot, or point within the entre of the circle, from of the circle, from which the m.m. cannot err, if he believes an so acts, etc." Manly P. Hall (1972) also states,

> The third ventricle is a vaulted chamber of initiation. Around it sits three kings, three great centers of life and power: the pituitary body, the pineal gland, and the optic thalamus. The third ventricle is supposed to be the seat of the soul, located between the eyes and just above the root of the nose. It is herethat the jewels are placed in the forehead of the Buddhas, and it is also from this point that the serpent rose from the crown of the ancient Egyptians.

Several of the Mystery Schools (African Univerisities) teach that this is the seat of Jehovah (God) in the human body.   Black Dot is the center of one's mind, the higher self and the center of all consciousness. It is that central, personal essence of ourselves that is immortal, unmoved by time or space. When clairvoyantly studying the body of man that little point always shows up as a black dot and cannot be analyzed.   An excellent review of the ancient African's definition of the nine attributes of the soul can be found in Dr. James' book, *Stolen Legacy.*

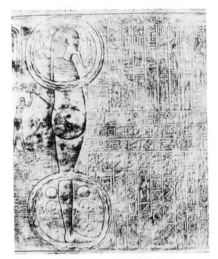

Fig. 10 Uraeus, vol. 3

The picture above is from the wall of King Tut's tomb and depicts a human with a serpent surrounding the head, higher self and a serpent surrounding the lower body, lower self. The lower self is the ego, personal I, and has awareness of only the concrete level of the mind, awareness of the five physical senses. There are at least six other levels of reality that the mental slave does not recognize: (2) physical body-mineral consciousness, (3) vital body-etheric body-mineral consciousness (4) desire, emotional/ astral body-vegetable consciousness, (5) link between the lower mind (self) and higher mind (self), (6) univeral will-cosmic consciousness (Black Gnostic Studies, 1967).   Another view of the levels of the unconscious, infinite memory is given by Roberto Assagioli (1965). The lower unconscious contains elementary psychological actitivies which coordinates bodily functions, fundamental drives, primitive urges, complexes, inferior imagination, uncontrolled parapsychological processes (uncontrolled ESP), pathological manifestations such as phobias, obsessions, compulsive urges, paranoid delusions and repressed/suppressed memories from one's own lifetime. Middle unconscious is where ideas are easily available and recallable. Higher unconscious contains higher inituitions, inspirations, altruistic love, genius, illumination, latent higher psychic functions and spiritual energies. The field of consciousness contains that part of reality that we are currently aware of at this moment: consious self or I is the whole self of which the I or conscious self is only a part of; collective unconscious is the ancient memories of past life, the psychic net of the cosmos, primeval waters, Ptah, and the word. Few Africans today can appreciate the levels of the unconsious within themselves because they seldom know themselves well enough. Even though we all sleep one-third of our lives, dream and see parts of our unconscious, we seldom know. People of years past, strange animals, visions of the future all fill our individual dreams. We don't even know the language of our minds. Although we have been in an oppressed condition for 400 years, our African roots and highly advanced African contributions are alive today in the collective unconscious level of our mind. For example, we may see snakes in our dreams, and mistakenly read that as a bad omen, neglecting the original African meaning because our oppressor mistakenly defines snakes as evil. Africans must know their own history for it is needed to correctly read the language of their own mind, language that is still expressing unconscious ideas in Ancient African tongue. *African History is essential for African Mental Health and the transformation of African Mental Slaves into African Masters.*

Inner Vision, Intuition, Separation of the Sexes

Inner vision occurs as intuition on the spiritual level of consciousness. Intuition, the direct perception of reality, occurs with a developed pineal. A developed pineal increases melatonin output when there is a balance between the male and female parts of one's consciousness. The male part of consciousness is the left brain and seat of logical linear thought. The female part of consciousness is the right brain and seat of intuitive non-linear thought. To know one's self is to become initimate, in a psychological sense, with one's self, and to peer into one's unconscious during R.E.M. (dream) where there occurs pineal and clitoral erection, called psychological intimacy. There is evidence that the early life forms that became humans (Devonian fishes 500 million years ago) had skulls with two eyes in front and two eyes in the rear. It was an androgynous being. In later years the sexes physically separated. The eyes in the rear withdrew into the brain to become the physical pineal gland. The pineal gland in some lizards still exist as a third eye conveying visual images (King, 1977).   Thus, one can appreciate the profound anatomy, chemistry, psychology and endocrinology behind the Ancient African statement that the transformative process produced inner vision (pineal gland, third eye) and illumination (intuition, inner light, perception) (Ukodari, 1978; URAEUS Vol. 1, 1978).

URAEUS PARTS I-IV SUMMARY

Long ago African scientists defined how the chains of mental slavery could be broken and mastership achieved. This was referred to as a transformative process through the development of one's mind. One had to develop mind (seven levels of consciousness) and move energy from the base of the spinal column, sex organs, to the top of the brain (pineal-pituary gland, third eye). This movement up the snake-shaped spinal column was defined as the development of Uraeus, a serpent in the pineal and depicted in the forehead region of the African King's crown. Thus, knowing one's mind requires knowledge of African history. African history is critical to mental health as one must know the African meaning of ideas so that they will recognize ideas when they appear in their dreams, intuition, and logic.

Uraeus One defined, the present condition of Africans (mental slavery); Uraeus Two the African history of the snake symbol; Uraeus Three African psychology and Uraeus Four African structure of the mind (Amenta, unconscious).

The most important thing in the development of Uraeus and rebirth of the African mind is for one to know and study inner self. One must discover the seven levels of knowledge that are operative within us all. Know your dreams, feelings, sensations, logic, intuitions, visions, beauty and perfection. Treasure the temple (mind, body), African history, African science and African religion. Reclaim the ancient African methods of Uraeus development: 10 Virtues, 7 Liberal Arts, Memphite Theology and the Negative Confessions.

PART THREE

Chapter Eight

ESOTERIC FACTORS OF THE CRESS THEORY

T here is a huge difference between black and white. The black man and the white man are distinctly separate and unequal. There is a state of war between the two races that spans thousands of years and has extinct billions of lives. Seldom has this planet witnessed a confrontation, a war of such dimension. It is a true example of total war, that is at times subtle or overt, mental or physical. It is warfare raging through every form of human expression from art to politics and religion. No safe ground exists, no neutral territory, no fence to straddle, all of us are involved. The confrontation between black and white is a total war for survival. Without a doubt, the meaning of black vs. white confrontation must be understood by every human if we are not to be severely crippled, consumed or destroyed.

These statements I make with deep emotion and logic. To be open to an analysis of new and provocative insights is the readers choice. Internalizing these ideas will cause much pain. It will be the pain of confronting old habits, old attitudes, traditions, defenses and personal insecurities. It will be the pain of confronting psychological scars and physical scars that are thought merely to cover wounds and prevent healing. It is on the most basic issue of black and white that we now engage.

The issue of black and white must be discussed on an exoteric and esoteric level. Exoteric means that which is superficially apparent, the outer appearance, lunar, the "is." Esoteric means that which is not superficially apparent, hidden from view, solar, the "why." The esoteric is the internal structure and support upon which the exoteric outer covering rests. The exoteric factors of color confrontation have to do with observations and verification of "what is" the behavior of whites and blacks together, while esoteric factors of black and white behavior together, consists of answers to "why" the "what is" behavior exists.

In, *The Cress Theory of Color Confrontaion and Racism (White Supremacy)* by Dr. Frances Cress Welsing, there is a clear outline of the exoteric factors of color confrontation. She observed that "at least three-quarters of the people are non-white and that the totality of the non-white majority population has been subjected to domination over the entirety of their lives, either directly or indirectly, by a tiny minority of the world's people who classify themselves as white. From this significant observation additional studies were made concerning the motivational forces that would explain individual and group behavior in black vs. white color confrontation settings. Some of the findings were:

(1) Reaction Formation - Going to the opposite extreme; over compensation for unacceptable impulses, for example: (a) whites openly despising blacks and making great use of skin coloring cosmetics or suntaning. (b) Elaboration of white supremacy myths.

(2) Projection - Attributing one's own thoughts or impulses to another person. (a) White's fear of anti-white hatred by blacks, (b) White's desire for black sexual relationships, (c) Universal white selective mutilation of black sex organs during lynchings.

(3) Displacement - A change in the object by which an instinctual drive is to be satisfied; shifting the emotional component from one object or idea to another, i.e. (a) Focus on the size of the black man's sex organ; (b) White culture degrading of sex in thought and logic processes.

From these observations a functional definition of racial color confrontation was made: "The behavior syndrome of individual and collective inferiority and numerical inadequacy which includes patterns of thought and action as seen in members of the white organization."

Thus, the observations were made that people without melanin or skin pigment possessed a distinctly different mental behavioral complex than pigment containing people. Then, too, we must ask the next question, the esoteric question, why is skin pigment so important that people who lack skin pigment feel parenthetically inferior?

In regard to esoteric factors of skin pigment, several of the most important are:

(1) Maintenance of body defense mechanisms against disease.
(2) Sexual reproduction
(3) Body energy metabolism
(4) Extrasensory states of perception

Skin Color

In the human there are several different genes that determine skin color (Stern, 1953; Livingstone, 1969; Harrison and Owen, 1964). The genes that determine skin color are different than the genes that determine the color of the hair and eyes. Skin color is determined by the skin color pigment melanin. Melanin is produced in cells named melanocytes, cells that originate from the neural crest (embryonic structure from which the brain and nervous system develops) (Du Shane, 1948; Rawles, 1948; Rawles, 1953).

The melanocytes, which greatly resemble nerve cells in appearance, move into the deep skin layers (dermis) of embryos by 10 to 12 weeks (Sagebiel, 1972). Inside the melanocytes, there are capsules named melanosomes which contain the actual melanin pigment, a protein polymer. Later, the melanin pigment is transferred from the melanocyte to regular skin cells, keratinocytes (Cruickshank, 1964; Cohen, 1968). Within the keratinocytes melanin is located around the cell nucleus to protect the nuclei's genetic material from destruction by ultraviolet sunlight radiation (290-320 nanometer wave length). The harmful effects of ultraviolet radiation on skin with less melanin are several and include accelerated aging and skin cancer (Daniels, 1972). All albino Cuna Indians living at the equator develop skin cancer by age seven (McFadden, 1961). All white children living in the New Guinea highlands on the equator also develop skin cancer before puberty (Daniels, 1972).

There are four major stages in melanosome development (Toda, 1968). A stage I melanosome is an immature vesicle without internal structure. A stage II melanosome is a vesicle with internal structure. A stage III melanosome contains some melanin, and a stage IV vesicle contains a full complement of melanin. Before irradiation of skin with ultraviolet sunlight, the melanocytes of whites contain only a few stage IV melanosomes (melanosomes with a full complement of melanin) regardless of the coloration of the white person's skin. In very pale whites there are few of the stage II and stage III melanosomes (Szabo, 1972). After irradiation with ultraviolet, white skin contains some melanosomes in all stages of development. In contrast, melanocytes of brown (mongoloid) and black skin are filled with stage IV melanosomes before irradiation with ultraviolet, with a small number of stage II and stage III melanosomes. The importance of these findings is that white skin contains less melanin because of the melanosomes are far less active without sunlight.

Not only does white skin contain less melanin, but the melanin that is present is the skin is less effective because of the manner in which it is distributed. In whites and browns, there are melanosome complexes composed of several melanosomes clumped together within the keratnocytes, whereas in blacks, most melanosomes are present as single units (Szabo, 1972). A distribution of individual units provides more uniform color and protection than a distribution of complexes.

Therefore, black skin, when exposed to sunlight, has two advantages compared to white skin. First, black skin contains more melanin and the melanin is present as a uniform protective layer, protecting keratnocyte nuclei from accelerated aging and skin cancer.

Body Immunologic Defense Mechanisms

There is considerable evidence that differences in skin color play a very important role in determining the function of the organs involved in immunologic defense mechanisms. First, we should consider the relationship of the pineal gland and melanin as shown in Table I and (Riley, 1972). Though genetics determines the base line and basic level of melanin in the skin before irradiation, it is the pineal that determines the state of melanin production with sunlight. Higher levels of MSH produce higher levels of melanin. However, the pineal gland is calcified in only 5% of the black population as compared to 30-70% in white population (Daramula, 1972). The same calcification differences have been found in the Japanese as compared to whites (Chiba, 1948). Thus, it is clear from the earlier finding, that white skin contains few mature stage IV melanosomes, and that this is the result of calcified pineal glands secreting less melatonin which is needed to activate the immature melanosomes to evolve into mature melanosomes. Black pineals, by containing less calcium, secrete more melatonin and produce more MSH.

The secretion of MSH is extremely important for many reasons. Wasserman (1965) has suggested that darkening of the skin produces hyperactivity of the reticulo-endothelial system and a decreased adrenocortical activity. Wasserman cites three sources of evidence: (1) Africans and American Negroes have a smaller adrenal cortex in relation to the adrenal medulla than do whites. (2) There is a lesser 17-hydroxy corticoid excretion in Africans, Malaysians and Indians and lesser postoperative increase in Africans. (3) Leukocyte counts of Africans tend to be low with a high number of lymphocytes. These findings are not unusual since low levels of ACTH are known to produce the above listed findings. The chemical structure of MSH is similar enough to ACTH to turn off the feedback control of ACTH secretion while different enough to not produce the same effects of ACTH (Williams, 1968). Without ACTH suppression, the reticuloendothelial system (lymphocytes) becomes more active. It is the reticuloedothelial system which is largely responsible for body's defenses against diseases, such as cancer. Skin color promotes health by reinforcing the reticuloendothelial system defenses against the spread of infection.

The pineal glands of persons dying with cancer have higher calcium content than those dying from other causes (Rodin, 1967). Engel (1933, 1934, 1935) found extracts of pineal tissue to inhibit the growth of some experimentally induced cancer in rats and mice. Other scientists have found an acceleration of the growth of cancer in animals with their pineal removed (Katagirs, 1944; Rodin, 1963; Das Gupta, 1967). When pineal extracts or melatonin has been used in humans, a temporary relief of symptoms of cancer has been found (Saunder, 1952; Lerner, 1960; Hofstatter, 1959).

Skin color also promotes the maintenance of sexual reproductive organs. The fourth decade in females is the only time in which there is no calcification of pineals (Daramula, 1972). The fourth decade is the period of menopause, a time in which the ovaries cease producing estrogen. If we take a lack of pineal calcification to be an indication of high pineal activity and production of high levels of MSH, then we see

TABLE I

Name & Source	Synonyms	Principle Actions
Anterior Lobe TSH	Thyroid stimulating hormone, thyrotropin	Stimulates thyroid growth and secretion
ACTH	Adrenocorticotropic hormone, corticotropin	Stimulates adrenacortical growth and secretion
Growth Hormone	GH, somatropin, STH	Accelerates body growth
FSH	follicle-stimulating hormone	Stimulates ovarian follicle growth in female and spermatogenesis in males
LH	Lutrinizing hormone, interstitial cell- stimulating hormone, CSH, prolan B, ovulating hormone	Stimulates ovulation and lute- inization of ovarian follicles in females and testosterone secretion in males
Prolactin	Luteotropic hormone LTH, luteotropin lactogenic hormone, mammotropin	Stimulates secretion of milk and maternal behavior. Main- tains corpus luteum in female rodents but apparently not in other species.
Intermediate Lobe MSH	Melanocyte-stimulating hormones, melanotrpins, intermedins	Expand melanophores
Posterior Lobe Vasopressin	Antidiuretic hormone	Promotes water retention

The Pituitary Gland: Review of Medical Physiology, by Gonong, William (1967)

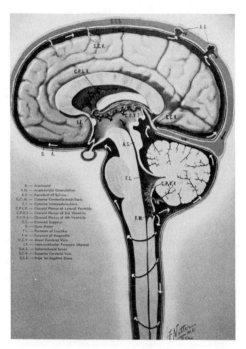

Fig. 11 Functional Neuroanatomy, Netter, Frank
(Ciba Collections of Medical Illustrations, v.1,)

that MSH acts to increase the levels of estrogens. When there are high levels of estrogen, there is a reflex feedback of decreased MSH. Then, too, it is well-known that low levels of estrogen stimulating gonodtropins produced by the pituitary are secreted in increased levels when the pineal secretes in increased levels (Chessman, 1970). Another interesting relationship is that the spleen, which is a major site of the reticuloendothelial system, partially blocks the gonadotropin released by the pituatary (Trentini, 1971).

Energy Metabolism

Skin color promotes lipid metabolism rather than carbohydrate metabolism. In Table I we see that MSH acts through the adenyl cyclase-cyclic AMP system. As a result, increased levels of MSH produce increased levels of cyclic 3', 5' - AMP. Cyclic 3', 5' AMP activates lipase which converts glyceride to fatty acids (Williams, 1968). With an increase in the amount of fatty acids and a decrease availability of carbohydrates, there is an increased metabolism of fatty acids (Randle, 1964). This is very important as fats contain twice the amount of energy for the same weight as carbohydrates. Then, too, the brain of new born children metabolates fats only. Thus, the question arises whether the fats, being a more efficient metabolic food for the brain, may be the natural original food by which the brain operates best. If we consider the fact that fatty atherosclerotic heart disease is present in blacks eight times more frequently than in whites, the possibility exists that high carbohydrate diets may be the wrong diet for people whose skin color-pineal relationship predisposes fat metabolism. It is by fasting for periods greater that 48 hours that fat metabolism promoted. Then, too, eating meats may hamper fat metabolism as meat subcutaneous tissue contains many long-chain unsaturated fatty acids that fat metabolic pathways cannot adequately process.

Extrasensory Perception

Elevated levels of pineal MSH are strongly implicated in extrasensory perception and emotionality. The amino acid tyrosine, which is produced in the process of producing melanin, is also the precursor of coedine, murphine, mescaline, LSD, thyroxin, and norepinephrine (Riley, 1972). These are chemicals that range from the psychedelic drugs mescaline, L.S.D., D.M.T., through the euphoric addictive drugs morphine and coedine. The psychoactive drugs used to calm down psychotics who have altered states of consciousness or delusions (believing things that have no logical basis--"I am Jesus") and hallucinations (sensations with real things that correspond to sensations--"I see pink elephants") have a direct effect on the pineal-melanin system (Scott, 1972).

Black vs. White

It is clear that skin color is important and a result blacks and whites are distinctly separate and unequal. By lacking a predominance of skin color, white people have fewer defenses against diseases, less efficient body energy metabolism, reduced potential for extrasensory -emotional powers, and less viable organs for sexual reproduction.

This however, raises another question. If blacks have greater defenses against diseases, then why is there so much disease in the black population today? A likely answer is that the black man's body is out of balance because of inappropriate dietary habits. Although black bodies are geared for fat metabolism, they are currently in carbohydrate metabolism by virtue of diets that include meat-eating, non-fasting, and high carbohydrate intake.

For blacks, to understand the importance of skin color may mean to drastically change their diets and define what their potential is for extrasensory emotional powers. For whites, the color question may mean to deal realistically with physiological differences rather than ignore them, and occupying themselves with insecurity induced hatred for the black man. Ignoring the problem has never solved the problem.

We can say that the pain of confronting old habits is the pain of giving up the known old for the uncertain new. But we must change if old methods remain inadequate for future development. Our fear of new methods can best be overcome by careful analysis of new cultural life style systems and thorough study along exoteric and esoteric lines.

Chapter Nine

SYMBOLISM OF THE CROWN IN ANCIENT EGYPT

T he historical origin of the twin pillars of modern European-African psychiatry, biological psychiatry and psychoanalytic depth psychiatry, can be directly linked to a common historical parent, The Science of the Mind and Way of the Heart of ancient Egypt (Ghalioungui, 1973). This premise arose from the observation of the crown, jewels, and tableaux found in the tomb of the 18th dynasty pharoah Tut-ankh-amun (?-1349 B.C.) (Leek, 1972; Jochannan, 1978; Lamy, 1981; West, 1979).
These items of material evidence are excellent examples of symbolic references to a historical stream of ancient African philosophical thought that extends from the predynastic Egyptian period, Memphite cosmology, to dynastic Egypt and later postdynastic heirs of Egypt, Dogon cosmology. The evidence cited is not new, having been in the hands of investigators for over fifty years. Rather, it is the order in which the facts are arranged that is both new and very old, the meaning given to the evidence, an acknowledgement of a greater whole from which these ideas are abstracted. For it is an Afrocentric corpus of thought, an Afrocentric world view on the part of the investigator that appears to be an absolutely critical focus and tool of analysis in an examination of the crown, jewels, and tableaus of the Pharaoh Tut-ankh-amun. From such an analysis there may come an appreciation of more subtle issues relating to the pineal gland, melanin, light and depth psychology issues of the unconscious, dreams, and levels of consciousness.

The largely intact tomb of the Pharaoh Tut-ankh-Amun was discovered in 1922 by Howard Carter and excavated over a six year period (Leek, 1972; Jochannan, 1978; Romer, 1981). A diadem crown was found atop the Pharaoh's head, covered in linen wrappings that extended over the entire mummy. On the mummy was a golden mask that was placed within one coffin and then enclosed inside two successive shrines. The surface of each of the four were covered with elaborate tableaus.

The right side of the second tableau of the second shrine contains a scene of a serpent passing rays of light into the forehead of the first of six human figures of Pharaoh Tut-ankh-Amun. The next two human figures have rays of light entering their foreheads from a star anterior and above the head.   The last three human figures have stars passing rays of light from star to star, each star in all cases being directly over the head of each human figure.   In front of each of the six human figures are two columns with a human headed hawk-like bird standing atop two columns.   The bird stands in such a manner that its left foot rests atop the left column, the right foot rests on the right column and the body and human head of the bird is situated between the two columns (Piankoff, 1977; King, 1983).

Two of the jewels taken from the tomb of Tut-ankh-amun are symbolic replicas of the ancient Egyptian concept of the left eye and right eye (Lamy, 1981).   The replica of the left eye (back cover) is framed by a serpent wearing the crown of Lower Egypt at the left corner and a vulture wearing the crown of Upper Egypt at the right corner of the eye. The replica of the right eye (front cover) depicts a scrarab body of a hawk whose outstretched wings and front legs uphold a boat. Within the boat is an eye framed on each side by cobras with sun disks above each serpent's head.   Above the eye there is a crescent shaped moon containing a moon disc with the figures of the ibis-headed moon god Thoth wearing the moon disc, the king wearing the moon disc and sun god Ra wearing the sun with a serpent uraeus. Importantly, the god Thoth is on the left, the king in the center and the god Ra on the right.

There were at least five crowns found over the head of the Pharoah Tut-ank-Amun, in his tomb-diadem, mask, and three whole-body coffins. In all cases there is the same representation over the forehead of the king, the head of a serpent on the left and head of a vulture on the right.   Both of these objects were placed in the mid forehead location above the level of the eye brows. The crown closest to the head, the diadem, actually enclosed inside the mummy's linen wrappings, not only displays the midforehead serpent and bird but also the wave-form body of the serpent across the midline of the crown and of the skull.

Furthermore, the diadem crown had the head and body of two serpents attached at the back of the head with the head of the serpent positioned at about the site of the temple on each side. Upon unwrapping the successive line wrappings of the head of the Pharoah Tut-ankh-Amun, and after the diadem crown was removed there was found a golden serpent and bird crowning the mid-forehead location (Leek, 1972). The wings of the golden bird were outstretched and covered the frontal portion of the crown of the head. The body of the golden bird rest atop the center line of the crown of the head from front to back. Yet before the head of the pharaoh was unwrapped, the symbolic importance of the crown of the head was clearly defined by the ancient Egyptian priests by their placing an extra pad of linen on the top of the head. Last, directly on top of the pharaoh's head there was a skull-cap with golden beads at about the middle of the crown of the skull and two serpents with heads over the temple regions on each side respec-tively. It is well known and reported in European-African archaelogical literature that the serpent was used throughout Lower and Northern Egypt as a symbol of the Goddess Uatchet. This was the case particularly in the city of Per-Uatchet, the capital of the seventh nome. This city of Uraeus worship as well as the other sites of its worship were collectively known as Pe-tep, within which were two distinct divisions. The first group *Tep* was identified with Isis and Uatchet. Isis was the worshipped divinity. The other, Pe was identified with Horus and Uatchet. Horus was the primary deity. Uatchet was regarded as the goddess of the elements and months of the Egyptian year, Epiphi, and during later dynastic times, was given the name Ap-tavi. Thus, in time the serpent and crown with a projecting coiled serpent-like body became a political symbol for royal rulership of Lower Egypt.

In a similar fashion the vulture became a symbol for royal rulership of Southern or Upper Egypt (Budge, 1969). Nekhebet was the vulture Goddess of the South. She was worshipped by the Egyptians throughout Upper Egypt in the city of Nekhebet, which was the capital of the third nome. This same city was called Eilethyiaspolis and "Civitas Lucinae," by the Greeks and romans respectively. The shrine of the Goddess Nekhebet, is presently located in the Arab village of El-Kab. Nekhebet was also believed to be the daughter of Sun God Ra.

Following the unification of Upper and Lower Egypt by the Southern Egyptian Pharaoh Narmer (4000?, 3200 B.C.E.) all rulers of unified

Egypt wore the composite crown of Egypt.   The crown contained the bulbous top of Upper Egypt and the coil of the crown of Lower Egypt.   Certainly his was a great political event and even greater psychological achievement to develop a real unified sense of shared commonality, purpose and philosophical oneness between two previously antagonistic groups of Africans.   Clearly, there is a strong suggestion of a similar process having taken place earlier in Upper Egypt with the collective name of Pe-Tep being derived from the unification of two distinct divisions of Pe and Tep.   Likewise, in Southern or Upper Egypt in pre-dynatic times there had been a unification of a least three distinct divisions that worshipped the Gods Nekhebet, Sun God Ra, and the goddess Hathor.   It is of utmost importance that we consider the political and military significance of such unification events and acknowledge the psychological basis that must have allowed mutual respect, synthesis, and flourishing of all parties involved.   With this in mind, one may consider the symbolism of the crown of ancient Egypt.   For, in reviewing the crown, shrine tableau, and jewels it is readily apparent that the serpent of Lower Egypt and the vulture of Upper Egypt were found to have other symbolic meanings than just political rulership over the two geo-political units of Southern and Northern Egypt.   From a psychoanalytic perspective a symbol has been defined as an act or object that represents an unconscious desire which has been repressed or automatically forgotten without ever having become conscious to the observer (Guralink, 1968).   Symbols are inherently linked to deep spontaneous unconscious psychological processes.   In contrast, signs are linked to largely conscious processes in which the observer consiously and arbitrarily allows one thing to stand for another.   For example, in the case of a sign, ten different observers may use ten different signs to represent the same item.   In the case of a symbol, different observers may use the same symbol to represent a wide variety of classes of objects.   The serpent and vulture found in the central mid forehead position of the crown of Tut-ankh-Amun is a symbol in that it is linked to deep unconscious psychological processes that tie together seemingly unrelated items from a conscious perspective such as religion, political unification, rulership, sun, moon, psychology and brain anatomy.   To appreciate the psychological concept of symbolism it may be helpful to consider the issues of projection, collective unconscious, in that the word symbol is partially derived from the word *ballein,* to throw. The process, to throw, speaks of a psychological state "projection," the unconscious act of ascribing to or throwing upon external things one's own ideas or impulses. What one sees externally as a good symbol to link together several seemingly unrelated items comes from a pre-existing unconscious memory of an idea. There exists many different levels of the unconscious, one of which is the collective unconscious which contains the genetic memory of all that was ever known or experienced by one's ancestors. The concepts of mind, soul and spirit were so important that this triune concept was a constant theme throughout many layers of their philosophical thought and scientific disciplines. There was a division of many things into three. There were three grades of students (neophyte, intelligence, sons of light) (James, 1976).   Temple architecture comprised an outer court for public congregations, a middle hall for priests and nobles, and an inner middle chamber, adytum, Holy of Holies, solely used by the high priest. There was the Goddess Isis (female), God Osiris (male), and God Horus (child, union of opposites). An entrance to the temple was formed by a doorway in which the left pillar represented the masculine energy of creation, right pillar the feminine energy of creation, and the arch way that joined the two pillars represented the soul with the words written upon it, "Man Know Thy Self." Thus, it is likely that Pharoah Tut-ankh-Amuns tomb with three successive coffins enclosed within a quartzite sarcophagus are symbolic replicas of the soul, spirit, mind and body (the last being the quartzite sarcophagus). The three shrines which successively enclosed the coffins and sarcophagus may represent the freedom of the spirit, soul and mind of humans following the death of the physical body. "The Egyptian Mystery System," as George James in his book *Stolen Legacy* points out, "had as its most important object, the deification of man, and taught that the soul of man, if liberated from its bodily fetters could enable him to become godlike, see the Gods in this life, attain inner vision and hold communion with the Immortals." It sought, "the liberation of the mind from its finite consciousness, when it becomes one and is identified with the Infinite. This liberation was not only freedom of the soul from bodily impediments, but also from the wheel of reincarnation or rebirth. It involved a process of discipline (several liberal arts) or purification (ten virtues, negative confessions, *Book of the Coming Fourth by Day*) both for the body and soul." James further cited nine aspects of the soul as defined by the ancient Egyptians, of which four are central to the concept of spirit *(Khu)*, soul *(Ba)*, mind *(Ka)*, and body *(Khat)*. "The *Ka* is the abstract personality of the man to whom it belongs. It possesses the form and attributes of a man with power of locomotion, omnipresence and ability to receive nourishment like a man. It is equivalent to (Eidolon), i.e., image; the *Khat,* i.e, the heart-soul, dwells in the *Ka* and sometimes alongside it, in order to supply it with air and food. It has the power of metamorphosis and changes its form at will; and the *Khu,* i.e., spiritual soul, is immortal. It is also closely associated with the *Ba* (heart-soul), and is an Etheral Being." From these considerations it is possible that symbols not only arise from the deep unconscious of one's own present historical life, shared experience of one's genetic ancestors (Ba), but also the past reincarnation of one's Khu (spirit).

Further, it is interesting to observe in the tomb of Tut-ankh-Amun the jewels of the lateral eyes, for the moon rose on the side of the left eye as the sun descended on the side of the right eye, a position that can only occur if one is facing south, towards the Great Lakes ancestral homelands of the ancient Egyptians, Khui Land, and place of origin of those who later unified Egypt through military might, politics, but most of all knowledge.

One should consider even deeper questions by examining the crown, jewels and tableau from the tomb of pharoah Tut-ankh-Amun. Could it be that these African people gave no thought to the symbolism of their own skin color in response to the radiation of the sun and the moon? What were the discoveries of these worshippers of the sun and moon and what was the relationship of the human form to light? The scene of the tableau clearly poses such questions where we see the serpent passing ray of light into a midforehead site of the human figure, and stars passing rays of light into a midforehead site of two successive human figures. This is a crucial item of physical evidence relative to African knowledge of biological psychiatry and depth psychiatry thousands of years before the rediscovery of the same knowledge by Europeans. This scene was probably already ancient and well known by the Africans when placed inside the Pharaoh Tut-ankh-Amun's tomb in 1349 B.C.E., three thousand years before European scientists Axelrod and Lerner redis- covered, in the 1950, that the pineal was not a nonfunctional vestigal organ but an active brain endocrine gland that released the hormones melatonin and seratonin (Reiter, 1981; Wurtman, 1977; Smith, 1983; Carman, 1976; Moskovitz, 1978).

When we read of the discoveries of Greek scientists and philosophers from the time of Pharoah Amasis onward there exists the very great possibility that their discoveries were not their own but the teachings of their Egyptian professors. This would particularly be the case with Herophilos, so called discoverer of the pineal gland. Importantly, Herophilos is noted for localizing the soul in the brain's ventricular system. Yet, as we have seen upon viewing pictures of the unwrapping of Pharoah Tut-ankh-Amun's head it was the golden bird that laid across the top of the crown of the head (Leek, 1972). The bird's outstretched wings covered the front of the head and its body covered the center line of the head, which may have been a symbolic statement of the African knowledge of the location of the soul being in the brain's ventricular system. This is because the shape of the bird closely resembles the top-view appearance of the ventricular system, lateral ventricles are similar to the outstretched wings and the body resembles the third and fourth ventricles. The pineal gland is located anatomically at the posterior end of the third ventricle and the pituitary gland is present at the anterior end of third ventricle. Modern science has now discovered that though pineal hormones are released into the blood they are concentrated primarily in the cerebrospinal fluid (C.S.F.) that flows through the brain ventricular system (Barr, 1982). The third ventricle has long been called the vault of initiation. Certainly, it is most critical to consider that the ancient Egyptians not only knew of the psychological operation of what they term the spirit, soul, and mind but had also defined the physical location and perhaps physiological operation of this trinity.

Ancient Africans appear to have had knowledge of pineal anatomy, its psychological effects, and its physiological relationships with other parts of the brain structure. These Africans knew that the pineal contained chemical keys that could unlock various levels of consciousness and yield operative awareness of the person mind, soul and spirit. This triune concept of spirit, soul and mind appear to have been central concepts found throughout various layers of their educational system. The stated purpose of their educational system was to free the soul from the finite consciousness of the body. Thus, it is reasonable to expect that such a people would have developed an elaborate system of symbolism.

Chapter Ten

PYRAMID TEXTS: *Selected References to the Eye of Heru*

G eorge G.M. James, in his transformative work, *Stolen Legacy*
defined the Ancient Kemetic purpose of education was the deification of
man through a process of "salvation". Salvation was clearly seen as a
separation, and awakening of the soul or higher mind from the chains of
the lower mind, flesh, dense material body. Upon awakening, one attained
freedom of the soul with full use of unlimited powers. It is at this point that
one did converse and communicate with the gods in order to return to one's
own latent godhood state of being. Thus, for these Africans the quest for
spirituality, attainment of a free and operative soul or higher mind was the
feature that gave value, and meaning to life.

The ancient African educational system was comprised of three grades.
Neophyte, the first grade achieved by the entering student. Intelligence,
was the second grade in which one came closer to freeing the soul as shown
by the attainment of inner vision, nous or mind. Sons of Light, the third
grade, and final stage of development, was so clear and all encompassing
that one actually experienced unity with light, total vision. The proof of
attainment of the Intelligence or Sons of Light was the expression of inner
vision. Thus, the educational process of these ancient Africans of Kemet
was a process of developing the vision of the inner eye, higher mind,
spirituality. In an attempt to seek some small measure of understanding of
the extraordinary operative inner vision of our African ancestors we will
review the great works of the Nile Valley: the Pyramid Text of the Old
King (3200-2100 B.C.E.), Coffin Texts of the Middle Kingdom (2100-
1675 B.C.E.), and the New Kingdom version of the Book of the Coming
Forth By Day (Book of the Dead, 1600-718 B.C.E.) and other texts such
as the *Ptolemic Edfu Texts* at the end of the dynastic age (332-30 B.C.E.).

Literature references particularly in the Coffin Texts and Pyramid Texts, are both extensive and beautifully written illustrations of the linkage between the Eye of Heru and the Kemite concept of the soul. This particular section will review selected references from the Pyramid Texts that pertain to the Eye of Heru as the organ of inner vision. Although discussion of the Great Kemetic Books will require many volumes to do it justice, I will attempt to give a brief review summarizing key concepts in the texts.

The Eye of Heru, Forehead Location and Relationship to Sunlight-Pyramid Text of the Old Kingdom (3200-2100 B.C.E)

Sun and starlight was directly linked to the Eye of Heru in the Pyramid text reference of Utterance 523, "May the sky make the sunlight strong for you, may you rise up to the sky as the Eye of Ra, may you stand at the left Eye of Heru where the speech of the gods is heard. Stand up at the head of the spirits as Heru stood at the head of the living;

Utterance 422 confirms the relationship between the Eye of Heru and the soul.
"O King, the Eye of Heru comes to you, it addresses you; your soul which is among the gods comes to you, your power which is among the spirits comes to you. The son has protected this king from his foes, May you arise O King, protected and provided as a god, equipped with the form of Wosir upon the throne of the foremost Westeners; may you do what he wanted to do among spirits, the Imperishable Star.

The relationship of the Eye of Heru to the ascension to higher levels of reality is found in Utterance 689. Geb has raised on high the potent (?) Eye of Heru which is on the hands of his great souls and upon ordinary souls. Turn your head that you may see Heru, for he has sat down and judgement comes to pass. Aset comes, having grasped her breast because of her vindicated son, and the King has found the Eye of Heru, this one finds the Eye of Heru, to whom her head has been given, and she has acted as a frontal on the brow of Re, who is as aggressive as a crocodile (?), follow the Eye of Heru to the sky, to the stars of the sky...who shall beseech Heru because of his Eye. O Shu, supporter of Nut, raise the Eye of Heru to the sky, to the stars of the sky, since Heru sits on this iron throne of his...who shall beseech Heru because of his Eye.

The comparison of the Eye of Heru to sunlight and starlight is confirmed in Utterance 639.
O Wosir the King, take the Eye of the living Heru that you may see with it. O Wosir the King, may your vision be cleared by means of the light. O Wosir the King, may your vision be brightened by the dawn. O Wosir the King, I give to you the Eye of Heru when Ra gives it. O Wosir the King, I put forth to you the Eye of Heru on that you may see with it.

These Utterances describe the purifying power of the Eye of Heru as well as its colors, in relationship to the Black Dot (pupil), protective power, and forehead location .
O Wosir (Osiris) the King, may the intact Eye of Heru belong to you, the Eye of Heru being intact, intact! (Utt.29) O Wosir the King, Heru has filled you with his complete Eye. (Utt.31) Take the two Eyes of Heru, the black (left eye) and the white (right eye); take them to your forehead that they may illumine your face-the lifting up of a white jar and black jar. (Utt. 43); O Wosir the King, I bring to you the two Eyes of Heru, which dilate the heart....take the Eye of Heru, prevent it from being consumed. (Utt. 57J,K); O Wosir the King, take the pupil (Black Dot) which is in the Eye of Heru, for your mouth is split open by means of it-2 bowls of h2mw-wine. (Utt. 155); See among whom this King stands, the horns on his head being those of two wild bulls, for you are a black ram, the son of a black ewe, whom a white ewe bore, whom the four teats suckled. The blue-eye Horus comes against you, beware of the red-eyed Horus violent of power, whose might none can withstand! His messengers go, his couriers run, they bear tidings to Him whose arm is raised in the East of the going of this One in you, of whom Dwn-nwy says: He shall give orders to the fathers of the gods. (Utt.246)

A clear relationship between the Eye of Heru (soul), Jehewty (knowledge) and Setekh (ignorance) is present in Utterance 356. O King, Heru has come that he may seek you, he has caused Jehewty to turn back the followers of Setekh for you, and he has brought them to you altogether; he has driven back the heart of Setekh for you, for you are greater than he. You have gone forth in front on him, your nature is superior to his; Geb has seen your nature and has set you in your place. Geb has brought your two sisters to your side, namely Aset (Isis) and Nephthys; Heru has caused the gods to join you, so that they may be brotherly to you in your name of Snwt-shrines and not reject you in your name of "Two Conclaves." He has caused the gods to protect you, and Geb has put his sandal on the head of your foe, who flinches from you. Your son Heru has smitten him, he has wrested his eye from him and has given it to you; you have a soul by means of it, you have power by means of it at the head of the spirits. Heru has caused you to lay hold of your foes, and there is none of them who shall escape from you. Heru has a soul, and he recognizes his father in you in your name of "Soul of the King's litter," Nut has placed you as a god to Setekh in your name of "God," your mother Nut has spread herself over you in her name of St-pt; Heru has laid hold of Setekh and has set him under you on your behalf so that he may lift you up and quake beneath you as the earh quakes, you being holier that he in your name of "Sacred Land." Heru has caused you to examine him in his inmost parts, lest he escape from you; he has caused you to lay hold of him with your hand, lest he get away from you. O Wosir the King, Heru has protected you, he has acted on behalf of his spirit in you, so that you may be content in your name of Contented Spirit.

Utterance 524 further clarifies the relationship of the Eye of Heru to the sun god Ra and other gods.
I am cleansed with the purification which Heru performed for his Eye; I am Jehewty who protects you, I am not Setketh who carried it off; rejoice, you gods! Be joyful, you Enneads! O Heru, meet me, for I wear the White Crown, the Eye of Heru wherewith one is strong. Be joyful, you gods, over me when I ascend; my face is that of a jackal, my arms are those of a falcon, my wing feathers are those of Jehewty, and Geb causes me to fly up to the sky that I may take the Eye of Heru to him. I have removed your boundary, you dead, I have overstepped your landmarks, you obstructors who are under the hand of Wosir. I have blocked the roads of Seketh, I have escaped the messengers of Wosir and there is no god who can lay hold on me, there is no adversary who can oppose himself to my road, for I am Jehewty, the mightest of gods. Atum summons me to the sky, and I take the Eye of Heru to him. I am the son of Khnum, and there is no evil which I have done. Long may this word be in your sight, O Ra; hear it, O Bull of the Ennead! Open up my road, make my seat spacious at the head of the gods, that I may take the Eye of Heru to him and that I may cause to be reknit for him that which went forth from his head. I will cause him to see with both his intact eyes, by means of which he will make his foes pass away.

Heru has taken possession of his Eye and has given it to me. My savour is the savour of a god, the savour of the Eye of Heru is on my flesh, and I am pre-eminent possessing; I sit on your throne, you gods, and I am side by side with Atum between the Two Wands. I am he who prevents the gods from becoming weary in seeking the Eye of Heru; I searched for it in Pe, I found it in On, I took it from the head of Seketh in that place where they fought. O Heru, stretch out your arm to me; O Heru, take your Eye; may it go forth to you when I come to you. May the Eye of Heru come to you with me, upon me for ever.

Chapter Eleven

COFFIN TEXTS: *Selected References to the Eye of Heru*

I n this section selected references from the Coffin Texts of the Middle Kingdom (2100-1675 B.C.E.) will be reviewed, that relate to the vision of the soul, once liberated. We will analyze the question of whether such extraordinary powers of vision, and spiritual symbols can be reliably examined, reproduced and used in our current pursuit of transformation.

The Eye of Heru is the Eye of the Soul

316   What is this on the morning when this god comes? The shades shall not be judged, the plans of the gods shall not be carried out. Look with your eyes, you elder gods, who afore-time, came into existence with the ancetors, on this spirit who has come here. He has become a flame, he has come into the island of fire. I have betaken myself to him through fear of the firery blast of his mouth-so say the elders who are about the shrine. *Send out your soul, that it may see with its eyes; such is Horus when he has reappeared in glory and has fashioned his bodily Eye.* Behold, it is stronger than any of the gods, it has taken possession of the Hau-nebut, and it is more than any god. Is the sole Eye stronger than the gods? So say I to my father Atum. Strength has gone forth to me from your mouth, and it means that I have become her who is strongest among the gods, and Seth has fallen because of me, I have made his confederacy slip because of that account on which he wandered. I have stood on his bonds, the monthly festival was fashioned for me, the half monthly festival was celebrated for me, I taste nothing evil, like the Lord of the monthly festival, the monarch of eternity. I am

strong and sharp of flame, (even) she who closed the house because of the coiled one, and mine is the coil of my eye. I am Horus who lifted up his Eye, which appeared besouled, high and mighty; it consumes the river. Food offerings are around me, through that spirit who burns up any dead, male or female, who shall come opposing me.

The Soul is Loosened from the chains of the lower mind, body and transformed from the lower mind (Seth) to the operative higher mind (Eye of Heru).

105,II,112   Going out into the day and assuming human shape. *O Bull, I lift up your bonds, O Bull, I give you your loosened fetters;* O Bull, I am not grasped by Shu, I am not seized by the earth-gods, I am not driven off by Re....Osiris has said of me: Give me his bones that he may use limbs and gather together his body for himself; and my bones have been given to me, I have used my body and gathered my limbs together like the eating of my body. My body has been given to me like the Great Lady, it being fair in his presence, my eyes have been opened for me by the Eyeless One, my [ears (?)] have been opened for by Mhnt-wr, I have heard acclamation from the mouth of the Entourage. My mouth is that of a falcon, my throat is fresh, the lashings which were on my mouth have been removed, the coils which were on my entrails have been opened; I eat with my mouth, I defecate with my hinder parts, and the foulness, has gone out of my mouth. Raise yourself, O nurse of the land, (even) Geb, father of the five. O you god who ascend and descend, they speak against me; do not repeat the word, but remember what shall come (?).

Eye of Heru raises one up to the Upper Level of a God
845   Take the Eye of Horus and be pleased with it, put the Eye of Horus on your brow. O Horus who is N; take the Eye of Horus, for it belongs to you, it belongs to your body, put it on yourself, provide yourself with it, for it will provide you as a god, lift up what is on you which is on the brow of Horus.

Location of the Eye of Heru in the Forehead

97 *Going out into the Day. The doors are opened, the contracts (?) are sealed on my behalf (?), for I am Thoth, the trusty one. O Eye of Horus, take me with you, that I may cause the seeing of your insignia on the vertex of Re. O Atum, come, give to me the Eye of Horus, that I may take it and bring it in.*

856 *O N, take the Eye of Horus; prevent him from consuming it. O N, take the Eye of Horus, the garment of which the gods are afraid. O N, Horus has attached his Eye to your forehead for you in its name of 'Great of Magic'. O N, take that of which the gods are afraid just as they are afraid of Horus. O N, take the Eye of Horus against which Seth acted. O N, take the Eye of Horus, the half of which he saw in the hand of Seth when he snatched it. O N, take the Eye of Horus, some of which he stole. O N, let him be far from you. O N, take the Eye of Horus which hung from the hands of his children. O N, take the water which is in the Eye of Horus, do not let go of it.*

The location of the eye of Heru is clearly identified as being in the forehead. The midline of the forehead above the brow is the location of the pineal gland, a light sensitive organ that in early fish and lower vertebrate existed as an actual third and fourth eye on the back of the head. Modern reptiles such as the western fence lizard, the pineal gland exists as a parietal or third eye at the anterior, on top of the head.

This eye is also given the name "Great of Magic" referring to the power to organize lower states of matter and bring it into creation. Seth, the lower mind, acts against the use of the Eye of Horus. He can steal, hide or confuse the commander of the higher mind. The Eye of Heru was rescused from Seth by Horus in struggle. This refers to the need to be far removed from lower states of consciousness that are Seth-like, and to remain on the higher plane of the Eye of Heru. Children of Seth, the progeny of Seth or associated lower mind states also conspire to keep hidden the Eye of Heru, by involving the neophyte in endless repetive obsessional acts.

Sweet Eye of Horus

11   *O N, take the sweet Eye of Horus; I put it in your mouth for you. A portion of [white sht] grain, a portion of [green sht] grain, a scorching of wheat, a scorching of barley, a portion of [b33wt], a portion of [zizyphus fruit], a portion of [zizyphus bread], all kinds of sweet fruits and of fresh vegetables, all kinds of hnkt, halves of earth-almonds. I cause choice joints to come, I bring forepart meat from the offering-tales for N has purity.*

The Eye of Heru produces joy. Many fragrant sweet perfumes, sft-oil, hknw-oil, nhnm-oil, quality pine oil, myrrh, are all associated with the Eye of Horus. These are not only libations, but olfactory stimulants of inner vision, imagery. For example the pine tree is symbolically linked to the concept of a non-dying tree or evergreen, the tree of life. The name, pineal gland is derived from pine cone, because the pineal gland is shaped like a small pine cone. The pineal gland, Eye of Heru, unlocks the gate to seeing the primeval waters of life, Nun, the collective unconscious.

861   *Horus has put gold on his Eye. O Horus who is N, take the Eye of Horus on which he has put gold for it is yours forever.*

O Horus who is N, I cause the two Eyes of Horus to go up for you to your face, I place for you the pupils which are in the Eyes of Horus in you head, I place for you their [...] on you in their name of the Two Great of Magic.

O Horus who is N, Horus gives you his Eye, and it will gude you on the path, your throat will be opened by means of it, and the water in it is yours forever.

Gold here, is not referring to an item of great material value. It is a thing which does not tarnish or corrode with exposure to the elements, it endures. Gold is a symbolic reference to the level of seeing and the ability to envision deep timeless water of Nun elements out of which the everchanging superficial elements evolve. Additionally, gold or yellow is the color of the sun and the pineal gland releases one type of hormone (melatonin during the absence of sunlight. When we sleep and dream we can see in our dreams the realm of the inner world, NUN.

Strength of the Eye of Heru

670 *Hail to you, Eye of Horus! The whole of (?) the sky is given to you, the earth is given to you to its thickness and the snakes which are in it; Re has given to you those two knots of yours which are in front of the Cow, Thoth has given to you those two knots of yours which are in front of [...], Neith has given you those two knots of yours which are in front of the Ibis, Atum has given to you those two (rays of) light of yours which are in front of the Vulture, and every god in your retine is completed, spiritualized and equipped. Turn your face, that your face may be strong, that your horns may be strong, that your.....may be complete; it means that N will be among them.*

The reference to strength being drawn from the "two" is a critical one, in that the "two" on one level may refer to the feminine emotional, intuitive ideas and the masculine logical ideas, and on another level it may refer to the endless process of raising young, raw ideas (Sethian-like) into mature adult ideas, that are growth promoting. For an idea to become mature it must make common sense or community sense and feel right.

608 *Ho N! You are clad in the Eye of Horus which belongs to your body. Ho! I have given it to you, it having appeared and having been seen on your flesh and having been joind to your flesh in this its name of 'Red Linen'.*
You are clad in it in this its name of 'Cloth'.
You are great in it in this its name of 'Great One'.
Your face is bright by means of it in this its name of 'Bright One'.
It is joined to your flesh in this its name of 'Red Linen'.
Here comes Tayt.
Here comes Taytet.
Here comes the Eye of Horus which issued from the earth.
Here comes the netting of Isis.
Here comes the cloth of Nephthys.
Here comes the plaiting of Neith.
Here comes the woven stuff of the two Sisterly Companions.
Here comes what Ptah has worked in.

Here comes what Horus gave to his father Osiris to clothe him in.
Ho N! Provide yourself with the Eye of Horus which belongs to
your body. Provide yourself with the woven Eye of Horus.

The act of a spirit being cloth in a dense material body, even with an
opened Eye of Heru, refers to a limited totality of light or Nun that
pervades the universe. For example the netting of Isis may refer to the
material/physical rescue of a developing student from intense desire for
physical objects, such as, lust greed, laziness.

607   *As for him who would harm your father when weak, he will*
be against you, O Horus-Eye, and you will be against him, O
Horus-Eye, Your right Eye is the Night-bark, your left Eye is the
Day-bark: your two Eyes, [O Horus], which issued from Atum,
are Shu and Tefenet. What revolts them is that the hand of the
god should misuse them, and the emission of the god's shade
should be behind them, and his semen shall not enter into them.
I have removed the Day-bark because of your Eyes, O Horus, I
have put them in the Night-bark and I have put them in the Day-
bark for Horus of Manu. The Blind Ones, rich in fluid (?), bleary-
eyed, shortsighted, are at the feet of Horus of Manu, and they will
neither be swollen (?) nor wobble (?) under the fingers of Horus
of Manu.

The Eye of Heru (pineal gland), is a light sensitive organ. The pineal
releases into the blood stream the hormone serotonin during the day
and melatonin during the night to activate R.E.M., that phase of sleep
during which we can consciously recall our dreams, or inner vision into
the primeval waters of Nun, collective unconscious.

587   *I am the Bull of offerings, possessor of five loaves in the*
temple; three loaves are in the sky and two loaves are on earth.
I bathe in the pools of the Netherworld, I ascend to the place of
Shu belonging to the sky. What Seth detest is the Eye of Horus,
and I will not eat feces; what I detest is urine, and I will never drink
it, just as Seth detested the Eye of Horus after the judgement in
the great Prince-mansion which is On.

If one gives him to you, fighting will not be stopped, uproar will not be suppressed, the mottled cattle will not move about for themselves, Seth will swallow the Eye of Horus for himself after the judgement in the great Prince-mansion which is in On, and if you give this to me, there will be no coming into being or existing.

A key feature of the lower mind (Seth) is that it swallows the Eye of Heru or keeps the hidden Eye of Heru in the faeces to make the good appear bad. Once the Eye of Heru is swallowed there is no coming into being or existing. This refers to the blockage of creative ideas and the failure to use one's will to shape material matter into a form seen by the Eye of Heru. One literally stops pursuit of the highest dreams.

Re Atum is dead! Fire. Fire. I have come that I may be strong in your company. It is the Aggressor who joined the Scowler when Set who made the Eye of Darkness passes by. I am a destroyer with the Lord of robbery following me, I am he who passes by and splits open the darkness, and fire has no power over me as over anyone else who belongs to the night. The t-bird belongs to me, and I have split open the darkness.

Darkness is the absence of sunlight. Seth, the lower mind, makes it difficult to see one's dreams and visualize how to execute the fulfillment of one's highest dreams. Robbery by Seth or darkness is the theft of ideas that were meant to be brought into existence but the dreamer could not see light to do so.

335   I arrived at the Land of the Horizon-dwellers in the sky, I go out from the sacred portal. What is the Land of the Horizon-dwellers? What is this portal? They are the gods who are about the shrine. As for the sacred portal, it is the double doors from which Atum proceeded to the eastern horizon of the sky. O you who are in the Presence, give me your hands, for I am indeed one who has come into being among you. Who are those who are in the Presence? They are Hu and Sia who are with my father Atum the whole of every day. I restored the Eye after it had been injured on that day when the Rivals fought.

What is the fighting of the Rivals? It means the day in which Horus fought with Seth, when Horus carried off the testicles of Seth. It was Thoth who did this with his fingers. I raised the hair from the Sacred Eye at its time of wrath. What is the Sacred Eye at its time of wrath? Who raised the hair from it? It is the right Eye of Re when it was wroth with him after he had sent it on an errand. I was Thoth who raised the hair from it.

Land of the Horizon dwellers is a portal or doorway between two states of consciousness, one of the night and the other the day. Perhaps it is the goal of an educated African, with an open Eye of Heru, to beome operative in life as a Horizon dweller capable of drawing strength from endless waters (Nun) of the night to pattern and shape dense matter into perfect forms of the day.

157 Being assigned to provisions in the realm of the dead, being favoured and loved on earth, being the train of Horus and his followers, a mystery which men know in the house. Knowing the souls of Pe. O you Souls of the Night, Marsh-dwellers, Mendesians, you of the Fishnome, you of the Mansion of 'Ipw, Sunshade-bearers of the Adoration, who prepare beer of Nubia, do you know why Pe was given to Horus? You do not know it, but I know it.

It so happened that Re said to Horus: 'Let me see your Eye since this has happened to it'. He looked at it and said: 'Look at that (black) stroke with your hand covering up the sound Eye which is there. Horus looked at that stroke and said: 'Behold, I am seeing it as altogether white'. And that is how the oryx came into being. And Re said: 'Look again at yonder black pig'. And Horus looked at this black pig, and Horus cried out because of the condition of his injured eye, saying: 'Behold, my Eye is like that first would which Seth inflicted on my Eye', and Horus became unconscious in his presence. And Re said: 'The pig is detestable to Horus'. 'Would that he were well', said the gods. That is how the detestation of the pig came about for Horus's (sake) by the gods who are in the suite. Now when he was a child, his sacrificial animal was a pig before his Eye had suffered---

*suffered--Imsety, Hapy, Duamutef, Kebhsenuf, whose father is
the elder Horus and whose mother is Isis---and he said to Re:
'Give me two in Pe and Two in Nekhen from this second
company. May I be in my own right (?) an allotter of eternity, and
opener of everlasting, a queller of strife in this my name of Horus
who is on this pillar'.*

Pe was the seventh nome (city) of Kemet also called the fish nome.
Fish symbolises a life form that is at home in the waters of Nun and able
to move between portals. This may be symbolic of the human ability to
communicate between various archetypal neters in the collective unconscious mind (King, 1978; Faulkner, 1969; Obenga, 1989).

Souls of the night, perhaps refers to the ability to move in Blackness;
that which is beyond material, rational comprehension, that which is
hidden from the neophyte. Importantly, it is during the night that the
pineal gland releases melatonin (Ebling, 1989; Grant, 1976), a hormone
that inturn releases a pituitary, hormone (melanocytes, MSH) that in-
fluences black pigment in the skin, brain, heart and other organ sites.
Melatonin allows the entire body to be a doorway to light or information
exchange portal.

Marsh-dwellers may be symbolic of that state of consciousness, Eye
of Heru, that is semi-conscious; part dry land, part underwater. In this
state there is an easy flow of ideas between the collective unconscious
waters of Nun and land of the horizon dweller.

Sunshade bearer of the aduration may refer to the aduration of a fully
developed Eye of Heru, in which one can see one's own shadow;
Blackness, hidden complexes, and active lower Sethian states of consciousness that have now been purified and raised up to a god-like state
of being.

Pe, the seventh nome of Kemet was the city of worship of the serpent
goddess Uatchet in the city Per-Uatchet, the capital of the seventh
nome. This city of Uraeus worship including other sites were collectively known as Pe-Tep. Within Pe-Tep were two district divisions, the
first district was Tep identified as Isis. Uatchet (Isis) was the worshipped divinity. The second district was Pe, identified as Horus.
Uatchet (Horus) was the primary deity. Uatchet was regarded as the
goddess of the elements and the months of the Egyptian year (Epiphi).
During later dynastic times she was given the name Ap-Tavi.

The Serpent within the human form is the 33 vertebrae spinal column, atop which rests the head, two lateral eyes, and the inner eye-pineal gland (Eye of Heru). Development from the lower Sethian level of consciousness refers to the upward movement of a fish-life seed up the central canal of the spinal cord activating various endocrine glands along the way (ovaries, testicles, adrenals, thyroid, para-thyroid, thymus, pituitary, pineal gland. One's level of consciousness reflects the level of glandular activation. The uppermost pineal is the actual portal, and light transducer that initiates puberty, sexual maturation, and the Son of Light stage in which one experiences unity with light.

Pe was given to Horus by Re in compensation for the mutilation of his eye. This is the mystery. The Eye of Heru that was closed was opened, and activated by the life seed following its migration up the spinal column by a process of struggle. From the struggle, one developed knowledge of the seven liberal arts and ten virtues. This educational process simultaneously developed both right and left cortical hemispheres and produced a union of opposites and the opening of the third eye, Eye of Heru.

Of great importance is the clear statement that an injured Eye of Heru produced distorted vision where Black was mistaken for White. Furthermore, visualization of the Black pig through an injured eye produced a great pain similar to that cause when Seth inflicted a wound that injured the Eye. The pig may be a symbol of Seth, and the consumption of a state of consciousness that lacks judgement and discrimination in that it will take anything for food, including its own feces. It is also revealed that Horus, as a child, made the pig a sacrificial animal perhaps as a representation of development from childhood to adulthood. This growth increases the capacity for discrimination and judgement that one must have to open the Eye of Heru. Childhood states stay submerged in unhealthy conditions and lacks the will to permanently avoid negative consequences, because of the immediate pleasure the material body, (Sethian consciousness) experiences.

This important text provides insight into the Ancient Kemetic concept of the unconscious, developed over 4000 years ago, that provides the key link to modern depth psychiatry. Both the early 20th century pioneers of depth psychiatry, Sigmund Freud and Carl Jung, were intense students of Kemetic culture and philosophy throughout their professional careers. Sigmund Freud's (Sulloway, 1979) study and room where he conducted patient analysis were filled with Kemetic deity statutes, books and artifacts. A print of the African Pharoah Ramses II at Abu-Simbel hung over his analysis couch. He waited until the last year of his life, however, to publish, *Moses and Monotheism*, a book written 20 years earlier, that defined the African Origin of the Mosaic Law of his hebrew faith (Sulloway, 1979).

> *935   O N, I give you the Eye of Horus, because of which the gods were merciful. O N, I give you the Eye of Horus; betake yourself to it. O N, I give you the Eye of Horus which they guarded (?). O N, I give you the lesser Eye of Horus, of which Seth ate. O N, I give you the Eye of Horus, with which your mouth is opened. The pupil which is in the Eye of Horus, eat it. O N, I give you the Eye of Horus, and you will not be ill (?).*

The pupil is the Black Dot. The portal through which light passes through the Black doorway of the collective unconscious. Blackness appears as darkness to a Sethian lower mind consciousness. It evokes fear of the dense material matter that cannot be penetrated by a strictly logical mind. Blackness, or the veil of ISIS (consciousness) does invite communication by the way of the heart, highly evolved feeling tone and intuition. It is this faculty of the feeling tone, intuitive mind that is the hallmark of the African mind, immersed in symbolism and fluent in the language of time and space.

Summary

This review of the 4000 year old Coffin Texts of the Middle Kingdom and Pyramid Texts of the Old Kingdom well illustrates the process of Kemetic education, from lower (Sethian) states of consciousness to higher levels of consciousness (Eye of Heru). Growth was defined as movement from a childhood state that lacked discrimination, was prone to misinterprete Black for White, and participated in death inducing behavior that perpetuated unconscious states. Clearly these Africans fully realized that lower Sethian consciousness was the monster that would swallow the lesser eye of Heru and would falsely masquarade its limited powers to entrap the neophyte. Only through struggle is Heru able to take even the lesser eye away from Seth in order that he may open the greater Eye of Heru. Only through careful discrimination of the symbolic inner and outer worlds, spiritual food, perfume and material conditions, could the eye of Heru be opened. The opening of the Eye of Heru developed out of a struggle that purged and mounted ethical virtues, knowledge of the laws of nature and the will to pattern behavior and shape the material world in the image of perfection. Inner vision occurs in the awakening soul (Eye of Heru).

The great African texts reveal knowledge of the pineal gland that produced inner vision by release of a night time chemical key, serotonin, that unlocks the gates of the netherworld, collective unconscious, Nun. Melotonin, the pineal hormone that activates the human body melanic develops during exposure to light, sun, God (Ra). Section 157 of the Coffin Text presents biological issues related to the Eye of Heru (pineal gland) that have yet to be rediscovered by modern science.

Indeed, Africans knew that the Black Dot pupil is the infinite furtile womb for the birth of perfect male and female gods who possess unlimited extraordinary powers, and true unity with light.

Selected Bibliography

Akbar, Naim. (1985) Nile Valley Origins of the Science of the Mind. Nile Valley Civilizations Proceedings of the Nile Valley Conference Atlanta: Journal of African Civilizations, 2, 120-132.

Adeloye, A. (1974) Incidence of normal pineal gland calcification in skull roentgenograms of Black and White Americans. American Journal of Roentgenology and Radiation Therapy, 122:481-484.

Allen, Thomas George. (1974) The Book of the Dead or Going Forth By Day. Chicago: University Chicago Press.

Amaral, David G., Sinnamon, H.M. (1977) The Locus Coeruleus: Neubiology of a Central Noradrenergic Nucleus. *Progress in Neurobiology,* Vol. 9, 147-196

Barr, Frank (1982) Melanin and the Mind-Brain Problem. Berkeley: Institute for the Study of Consciousness.

Bazelon, Mary, Feinchel, Gerald M. (1968) Studies on Neuromelanin I, A Melanin System in the Human Adult Brainstem. *Neurology,* Vol. 18, 817-820.

Becker, Patricia T. (1981) *Science,* Vol. 212, 1415-1416.

Beeson, Paul B. (1968) Cecil-Loeb Textbook of Medicine. Philadelphia: W.B. Saunders Company.

Ben-Jochannan, Yosef. (1970) African Origins of the Major Western Religions. New York: Alekebu-lan Books Associates.

Ben-Jochannan, Yosef. (1971) Africa: Mother of Western Civilization. New York: Alkebu-lan Books Associates.

Ben-Jochannan, Yosef. (1972) Black Man of the Nile and his Family. New York: Alekebu-lan Books Associates.

Ben-Jochannan, Yosef. (1974) The Black Man's Religion and Extracts and Comments From the Holy Bible New York: Alkebu-lan Books Associates.

Ben-Jochannan, Yosef. (1983) We The Black Jews. New York: Alkebu-Lan Books, Associates.

Black Gnostic Studies (1970) Occult Philosophy, Lesson 1101. *Macrocosmic or Solar Key,* Los Angeles: Aquarian Spiritual Center.

Black Gnostic Studies (1970) Occult Philosophy, Lesson 1101. Microcosmic of Luner Key, Los Angeles: Aquarian Spiritual Center.

Black Gnostic Studies (1970) Occult Philosophy, Lesson 1101. *The Musical Key, Pattern is Equilibrium,* Los Angeles: Aquarian Spiritual Center.

Blois, M. S., (1969) Recent Developments in the Physics of Chemistry of Melanin Pigmentation. Pergamon Press.

Bodnar, R. J., Ackermann, P. F., (1978) Elevations in Noriceptive Thresholds Following Locus Coeruleus Lesions, Brain Research Bulletin, Vol 16, 331-336.

Bollingen Series XL (1957) Papyrus of Her-Uben B. Egyptian Religious Texts and Representations, 3, New York: Pantheaon Books.

Brier, Bob. (1980) Ancient Egyptian Magic. New York: William Marrow and Company

Budge, E. A. Wallis. (1969) The Gods of the Egyptians, Volumes I-II. New York: Dover Publications.

Budge, E. A. Wallis. (1967) The Book of the Dead. New York: Dover Publications.

Budge, E. A. Wallis. (1968) Amulets and Talismans. New York: University Publications.

Budge, E. A. Wallis. (1934) From Fetish to God in Ancient Egypt. London: Oxford University Press

Budge, E. A. Wallis. (1961) Osiris, Volumes I-II. New York: University Press.

Campbell, Bernard. (1976). Humankind Emerging. Boston: Little Brown & Company.

Cannon, W. B., *American Journal of Psychology,* 39:1927, 106-124

Cardonali, David P., Molecular Mechanisms of Neuroendocrine Integration in the Central Nervous System: An Approach Through the Study of the Pineal Gland and Its Innervating Sympathetic Pathway, Psychoneuroendocrinology, 8, 1, 1983.

Carlsson, A., (1978). Mechanism of Action of Neuroeptic Drugs. In Psychopharmacology a Generation of Progress. New York: Raven Press

Carman, John S., (1976) Negative Effects of Melantonin on Depression. American Journal of Psychiatry. 133:10, 1181.

Carruthers, Jacob H. (1984) Essays in Ancient Egyptian Studies. Los Angeles:Timbuktu Publishers.

Chessman, D.W. (1970) Isolation and characterization of a Gonado-tropin-inhibiting substance from the bovine pineal gland. Proc. Soc. Exp. Biol, Med., 133:1254-1256.

Chiba, M (1948) About the calcification of the pineal gland in the Japanese. Folia pychiatrica et neurologica japonica, 2:301-303.

Churchward, Albert. (1978). *The Signs and Symbols of Primodial Man.* Westport, Conn: Greenwood Press.

Churchward, Albert. (1924). The Origin and Evolution of Religion. New York: E.P. Dutton and Company

Churchward, Albert. (1921). The Origin and Evolution of the Human Race. London: George Allen & Unwin Ltd.

Cirlot, J.E. (1976) A Dictionary of Symbols. New York: Philosophical Library.

Cohen, J (1968) Study of pigment donation in vitro exp., Cell Res,. 50, 418.

Collins, Jean D. (1982) Can I Hold On To It. Uraeus, 2, 3:56.

Coppens, Yves, Howell, F. Clark. (1976) Earliest Man & Environments In the Lake Rudolf Basin. Chicago: University of Chicago Press.

Cotzias, G.C., (1974) Melanogenesis and Extra Pyramidal Diseases. Fed. Proc., 23:713.

Cox, George O., African Empires and Civilizations. New York: African Heritage Studies Publications.

Creel, D., O'Donnell, F.E. (1978). Visual System Anomalies in Human Ocular Albinos. Science. 201, 931

Creel, D., O'Donnell, F.E. (1980). Auditory Brainstem Anomalies in Human Albinos. Science. 209, 1253

Crowley, Aleister. (1970) *777.* New York: Samuel Weiser.

Cruickshank, C.N.D. (1972) Pigment donation in vitro J. Invest. Derm, 42, 183.

Csaba, G. (1974) The effect of pinealectomy on the para follicular cells of the rat throid gland. Acta anat., 88:137-146.

Daniels, F. (1972) Theories of the role of pigment in the evolution of human races, 13-22, New York:Appelton-Century Crofts.

Darmula, G.F., (1972) Neuroendocrinology, 9:41-57.

Das Gupta, T.K. (1967) Cancer Research, 27, 1306

Diop, Cheikh Anta. (1974) The African Origin of Civilization. New York: Lawrence Hill & Company.

Diop, Cheikh Anta. (1978) The Cultural Unity of Black Africa. New York: Lawrence Hill & Company.

Diop, Cheikh Anta (1982) Origin of the Ancient Egyptians. Journal of African Civilization, 4, 2:9-37.

Dushane, G.P., (1948). The development of pigment cells in vertebrates, 4, 1. New York Academy of Sciences. Special Publications

Edelstein, Leon M., (1971) Melanin: A Unique Biopolymer, Pathobiology Annual, 1, 309. New York: Appleton-Century-Crofts.

Ebling, F.J.P (1989) Pineal Melatonin Rhythms and the timing of puberty in mammals. Experienta, 45:946-965.

Faulkner, R. O., (1969) The Ancient Egyptian Coffin Texts. Oak Park, Illinois: Bolchazy-Carducci.

Faulkner, R. O., (1978) The Ancient Egyptian Coffin Texts Vol. I-III. Warminster, Wilts, England: Aris & Phillips Ltd.

Feinchel, Gerald M. (1968) Studies on Neuromelanin II: Melanin in the Brainstem of Infants and Children. Neurology, 18:817-820.

Filators, Jun, McGinnes, John. (1976) Thermal and Electronic Contributions to Switching in Melanins. *Biopolymers,* 15, 2309

Forrest, F.M. (1975). The Evolutionary Role of Neuromelanin. West Pharmacol So., 18, 205.

Forrest, F.M. (1972). On the Phylogenetic Origin of REM Sleep. West Pharmacol Soc., 15, 184.

Franklin, R. E., Gosling (1953) R., Nature. 171, 740.

Goodwin, David. (1979) Goodwin's Cabalistic Encyclopedia. Minneapolis: Llewellyn.

Grant, Kenneth (1976) Cults of the Shadow. New York: Samuel Weiser.

Giaule, Marcel, Conversations with Ogotemmeli. An Introduction to Dogon Religious Ideas. International African Institute. New York: Oxford Press.

Gilbert, Katherine (1976) Treasures of Tutankhamun, New York: Metropolitan Museum of Art.

Hall, Manly P., (1972) Man, The Grand Symbol of the Mysteries. Los Angeles: Philosophical Research Society.

Harrison, G.A. (1964) Studies on the inheritence of Human skin color. Ann. Human. Genet., 28:27-37.

Henderson, Joseph L., Oakes, Maude. (1963) The Wisdom of the Serpent. New York: George Braziller

Hinsie, L. E., Campbell, R. J., (1974) Psychiatric Dictionary. London: Oxford Press.

Hiroswa, Kazushige (1968) Electron Microscopic Studies on Pigment Granules in the Substania Nigra and Locus Coeruleus of the Japanese Monkey (Macaca Fusca Yuku) Zeitschift fur Zellforschung. 88:187-203.

Hobson, J. Allan (1977) The Brain as a Dream State Generator: An Activation-Synthesis Hypothesis of the the Dream Process. American Journal of Psychiatry, 133:10, 39.

Hoffstein, Robert M., (1975) The English Alphabet. New York: Kaedmon Publishing Co.

Holick, M.F. (1980) Photosynthesis of Previtamin D3 in Human Skin and the Physio-consequences. Science. 210, 10:203-205

Howey, M. Oldfield. (1955) The Encircled Serpent. New York: Richmond Co.

Huang, Y.H. (1975) Invivo Location and Destruction of the Locus Coeruleus in the Stumptail Macaque (Macaca Arctoides), Brain Research, 100, 257-262.

Jackson, John G., (1970) Introduction to African Civilizations. New York: University Books.

James, George G. M., (1976) Stolen Legacy. San Francisco: Julian Richardson.

Jones, Ernest. (1948) The Theory of Symbolism. Papers on Psychoanalysis. London: Ballidere, Tindall & Cox

Jouvet, M. (1965) Locus Coeruleus and Paradoxical Sleep. C.R. Soc. Biol. Paris, 159, 895-899.

Jouvet, M. (1969) Biogenic Amines and the States of Sleep, Science. 163, 32-41.

Jung, C.G. (1970) Dream Symbols of the Individuation Process, Papers From the Eranos Yearbooks., 4, 402-403. New York: Princeton University Press.

Kerenyl, C. (1959) Asklepios. New York: Bollingen Foundation

Khei, (1921) Rosicrucian Symbology. New York: Macoy Publishing and Masonic Supply Company.

King, Richard D., (1977) Pineal Gland Review. Los Angeles: Fanon Research and Development Center.

King, Richard D., (1977). Selected Annotated References. Los Angeles: Fanon Center Publication.

Kobayashi, Ronald. (1975) Biochemical Mapping of the Noradrenergic Projection from the Locus Coeruleus, Neurology.

Leakey, L.S.B., Olduval Gorge (1951-61). Fauna and Background. Cambridge: Cambridge University Press.

Leek, F. Filce, (1972) The Human Remains from the Tomb of Tutankamun, V. Tutankamun Tomb Series. Oxford: University Press, Griffith Institute.

Lewis, Charlton T., Harpers Latin Dictionary. New York: American Book Company

Litchtheim, Miriam (1980) Ancient Egyptian Literature, Vol III, The Late Period. Berkeley: University California Press

Livingstone, F.B. (1969) Polygenic models for the evolution of human skin color differences. Human Biology, 481-493.

"Macrocosmic Curriculum, Esoteric Tarot Chart," (1971). Los Angeles: Aquarian Spiritual Center-Black Gnostic Studies

"Macrocosmic Curriculum," (1967). Los Angeles: Aquarian Spiritual Center-Black Gnostic Studies

Marsden, C.D., (1961) Pigmentation in the Nucleus Substantia Nigra in Primates. Journal of Comparative Anatomy.

Maclean, Paul. Cerebral Evolution and Emotional and Scientific Basis in The Neurosciences, Second Study Program. New York: Rocker feller University Press.

Maclean, Paul The Triune Brain, Emotion and Scientific Basis in the neurosciences, second study program. New York: Rockerfeller Univeristy Press.

Massey, Gerald. (1974) The Typology of the Mythical Serpent. The Natural Genesis, Volume I. New York: Samuel Weiser.

McFadden, A.W. (1961) Skin disease in the Cuna Indians. Arch, Derm. 84:1013-1023.

Means, Sterling, M. (1945) Ethiopia: The Missing Link in African History.

Mess, B. (1975). Melatonin, Cerebrospinal Fluid, Pineal Gland Interrelationships, Brain-Endocrine Enteraction II. Karger, Basel.

Moskovitz, Charlene (1978) Levodoba-Induced Psychosis: A Kindling Phenomenon. American Journal Of Psychiatry 135:6, 669.

Moses, Harold. (1966) Light and Electron Microscopic Studies of Pigment in Human and Rhesus Monkey Substantia Nigra and Locus Coeruleus. *Anatomical Record*, 155, 167-184.

Moshe. (1980) The Black Race as Parent Stock, History, *The Bible and the Blackman*. Vol II, (2), 8.

Mtengwa, Al (1982) Hidden Knowledge. Uraeus, Los Angeles.

Muhammed, Elijah. (1974) Our Saviour Has Arrived. Chicago: Muhammed's Temple O Islam. No. 2.

Muller, W. Max., The Mythology of All Races, Egypt, Far East, 7. New York: Cooper Square Publishers, Inc.

Norelli-Bachelet, Partrizia. (1974) Symbols and the Question of Unity Holland: Service Publishers.

Obenga, Theophile (1989) African Philosophy of the Pharonic Period. Journal of African Civilizations, 10:286-324.

O'Donnell, F.E., Jr., (1978) Arch. Opthalmology.

Olswezski, J., (1964) Cytoarchitecture of the Human Brain, Stern and Birjelow. New York.

Oneda, Toshihiro (1969) Infrared Spectrometry of Locus Coeruleus and substania nigra pigments in the Human Brain. Brain Research Service. Reference Bibliography. 82:1-30.

Path, M.O., (1978) Phagocytosis of Light and Dark-Adapted Rod Outer Segments by Cultured Pigment Epithalium, Science, 203, 526.

Pathak, Madhukar. The Photobiology of Melanin Pigmentation in Human Skin.

Pearse, A.G.E.. (1976) Neuroedocrine Embryology and the APUD concept, Clinical Endocrinology.

Pearse, A.G.E., (1974) Endocrine Tumors of Neural Crest Origin: Neurolophomas, Apudomas and the APUD Concept. Medical Biology.

Pearse, A.G.E., (1973) The Apudomas. British Journal of Hospit Medicine, 617-624.

Pearse, A.G.E. (1969) The Cytochemistry and Ultrastructure of Poly-peptide hormone-producing cells of the APUD series and the Embryologic Physiologic Implications of the Concent. The Journal of Histochemistry and Cytochemistry. Vol 17. 5, 303-313.

Pearse, A.G.E. (1968) Common Cytochemical and Ultrastructural Characteristics of Cells Producing polypetide hormones (the APUD series and their relevance to thyroid and ultimobranchial cells and and calcitonin.

Pepper, C.M. (1980) Opiates and Opiod Peptides Hyperpolarize Locus Coeruleus Neurons in Vitro. Science, 209, 394-396.

Peterson, Christine. (1980) Science. 209, 394-396.

Pilling, J. (1977) Distribution of calcification within the pineal gland. British J. Radiology, 50:796-798.

Plato, Timeus, 22-23

Plummer, Gorden. (1970) The Mathematices of the Cosmic Mind: A Study in mathematical symbolism. Illinois: The Theosophical House

Quay, W. B. (1974) Pineal Chemistry. Springfield: Charles C. Thomas.

Randle, P.J. (1964) Regulation of glucose uptake by muscle. Effects of fatty acid, ketone bodies, pyruvate, diabetes and starvation on uptake and metabokic fat of glucose in rat heart and diaphram muscles. Biochemical Journal, 93:652.

Redmond, D.E. (1976) Behavioral Effects of Stimulation of the Nucleus Locus Coeruleus in the Stumptailed Monkey (Macaca Arctoides). Brain Research, 116, 502-510.

Redmond, D.E. Jr., New and Old Evidence for the Involvement of a Brain Norepinephrine System in Anxiety.

Riley, Vernon. (1972) Pigmentation: Its Genesis and Biologic Control New York: Appelton-Century-Crofts.

Romer, John (1981) Valley of the Kings. London: MichaeL Joseph Ltd.

Sagebiel, R. W. (1972) Ultrastructural identification of melanocytes in early human embryo. In Riley, v., ed., Pigmentation: Its genesis and bilogiccontrol, New York: Appelton-Century-Crofts.

Schouten, J.,(1967) The Rod and Serpent of Asklepios. New York: Elsevier Publishing Company

"Solar Key," (1970) Los Angeles: Aquarian Spiritual Center-Black Gnostic Studies

Scherer, H.J., Melanin Pigmentation of the Substania Nigra of Mammals.

Schneider, Walter. Association of D.N.A. with Melanin Granules. Journal of the National Cancer Institute, 55, 3, 665.

Schwaller de Lubicz, R.A. Symbols and the Symbolc, New York, Inner Traditions International.

Schwaller de Lubicz, R.A. The Temple in Man, New Yor, Inner Traditions International.

Scott, G.T. (1972) The action of psychoactive drugs on pigment cells of lower vertebrates. In Riley, v., ed., Pigmentation: Its genesis and biologic control. New York: Appelton-Century-Crofts.

Stern, C. (1953) Model estimates of the frequency of white and near white segregants in the American Negro. 4:281-298. Acta. Genet.

Szabo, G. (1967) Photobiology of melanogenesis: Cytolgical aspects with special reference to differences in racial coloration. In Montagna, W., ed., Advances in Biology of Skin. vol viii, The Pigmentary System, 379-396, New York: Pergamon Press.

Thompkins, Peter (1971) Secrets of the Great Pyramid. New York: Harper & Row, 203.

Toda, K.Y. (1968) Isolation of the intermediate "vesicles" during onto geny of melanosomes in embyonic chick retinal pigment epithelium. Fed. Proc., 27:722.

Ukodari, Malavor. (1978) The Personal Ascension of the Five Senses. URAEUS Vol. 1., 3, 10-14.

Van Woert, M.H. (1967) Spectroscopic Studies of Substantia Nigra Pigment in Human Subjects, J. of Neurochemistry, 14, 707-716.

Wassermann, H.P. (1965) Human pigmentation and environmental adaptation. 11:691-694, Arch. Environ. Health.

Wassermann, H.P., (1974) Ethnic Pigmentation: HIstorical, Physiological and Clinical Aspects. New York: Elseveir Publishing Co.

Watson, James D., (1970) Molecular Biology of the Gene. New York: W. A. Benjamin, Inc.

Welbourn, R.B. (1977) Current Status of the Apudmoas, Annals of Surgery, 185, 1-12.

Welsing, Francis Cress. (1970) The Cress Theory of Color Confrontation and Racism, (White Supremacy). Washington, D.C.: C. R. Publisher.

Williams, Chancellor. (1974) The Destruction of Black Civilization. Chicago: Third World Press.

Williams, R.H. (1968) The Pancrease. In Williams, R.H., ed., Textbook of endocrinology, 646, Philadelphia, PA.

Woodruffe, John. (1973) The Serpent Power. India: All India Press/
    M Ganesh & Company
Wurtman, Richard J., Moskowitz, Michael. (1977). The Pineal Organ
Part II. The New England Medical Journal. 296:24, 1977.
Zain, C. C., (1969) *Divination Chart.* Sacred Tarot. Los Angeles:
    The Church of Light.
Zorentzer, Steven F. (1975) The Locus Coeruleus: Its Possible Role
    in Memory Consolidation. *Physiology and Behavior,* 16:331-336.

List of Illustrations

1. Example of Black Dot Ancient Memory pulled from the collective
unconscious memory bank.
2. "Arat", meant cobra to the Ancient Egyptians. This is a hieroglyphic
depiction of the name Uraeus.
3. The relationship of Uraeus to the Egyptian God Ra is evident in that
it is the snake deity that is worshipped as a sign of sovereignty and
royalty.
4. Hieroglyphic description that depicts how Egyptians Kings placed the
Uraeus symbol before their names.
5. Uatchet was regarded as the goddess of the elements and months of
the Egyptian year. This is the numerical value for UATCHET.
6. The Shrine of Tut-ankh-Amun.
7. This figure shows the relationship between Uraeus and sunlight and
and depicts a serpent putting sunlight (rainbow spectrum of colors) into
the pineal forehead, and a star engaged in a similar operation.
8. An Egyptian Religious Text that shows a mummy with an erect black
penis.
9. Shows the location of the pineal gland as it relates to the African
understanding on godhood and mastership.

Index